MW01641764

As for me and my household,
we will serve the LORD.

Joshua 24:15

The Heart of a Loving Family
Copyright 2000 by Audrey Jeanne Roberts
ISBN: 0-310-98271-5

For more information on Audrey Jeanne Roberts, write to:
Audrey Jeanne's Expressions™
P.O. Box 157
Valley Center, CA 92082

Project Editor: Gwen Ellis
Assistant Editor: Molly Detweiler
Design: Bobby Strickland

Printed in China
00 01 02 03/HK/ 8 7 6 5 4 3 2 1

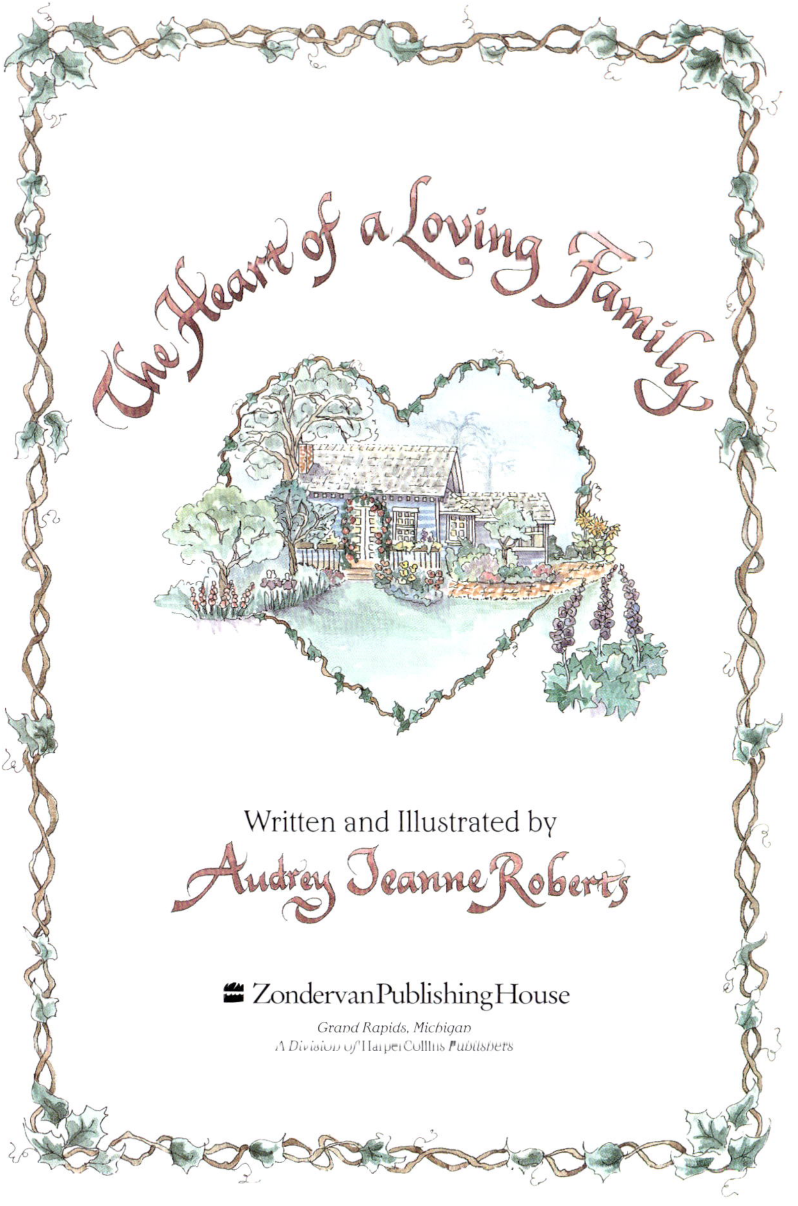

The Heart of a Loving Family

Written and Illustrated by

Audrey Jeanne Roberts

ZondervanPublishingHouse

Grand Rapids, Michigan

A Division of HarperCollins Publishers

Dear Friend,

Come journey with me and peek into the heart of a loving family—a family that isn't perfect, but one that truly enjoys each other! We'll share things the Lord has taught us about loving each other, as well as stories that will make you laugh and perhaps even touch your heart.

In my early years of parenting, I sought a way to stay home with my children and still provide a little extra money for expenses. In that process I rediscovered one of my childhood joys—calligraphy. To bring life to the letters, I began to experiment with watercolor and pen and ink and saw my sketches come alive.

Since the medium of calligraphy demands a message, I searched everywhere for special prose and poetry to deliver the message of home, family and friendship I wanted to communicate. I wanted to share the things of lasting value the Lord was teaching me in my day-to-day life as a wife, mother, homemaker and small business owner. I quickly discovered it wasn't easy to locate words that captured the essence of the emotions, relationships and values I wanted to share. Out of pure necessity, I began writing from my own life experience and saw my words touch hearts and change lives.

I began to share my work with others through home parties and craft shows. All too quickly the business outgrew my home. Under the Lord's guidance, I pursued the company's growth and saw it develop far beyond my wildest imagination. Since I loved being a homemaker so much, it was hard to understand why it was God's plan for the business to outgrow my home. Then my first husband, Jim, was diagnosed with terminal cancer and I was faced with the prospect of supporting my two precious daughters, alone. I began to understand.

Over the years the great majority of the work I produce for my product line, "Audrey Jeanne's Expressions," focuses on home and family and the events and emotions families experience every day. Now, I have the privilege of sharing my thoughts with you in a more intimate fashion. So take a moment, find a quiet corner, and join me as we discover The Heart of a Loving Family.

Yours truly,

Audrey Jeanne Roberts

Oak Haven Orchards
Valley Center, California

First, I want to thank my own "loving family" for allowing me to neglect them as the deadlines drew closer and closer. We've been through so much together; learning through it all that the Lord is utterly faithful. You're my favorite people on earth, and you all are a joy.

Thanks to my incredible husband, writing partner, art editor, best friend and spiritual leader, Stephen... I literally couldn't do it with out you.

I must acknowledge my wonderful team at Zondervan: Caroline Blauwkamp and Londa Alderink who saw the vision and ran with it. Gwen Ellis & Molly Detweiler, my editors who helped shape and smooth the book into its final form and all of the others who played a role behind the scenes... it's really fun having a team who's entire goal is to help you be a better you! Thank you all.

And to all the staff members at Audrey Jeanne's Expressions, thank you all for your faithful and tireless support. Not just for your continued day to day efforts at keeping the company running smoothly but, more importantly, for each of your prayers. Your loyalty and belief in our vision undergirds all we do.

Mostly, I thank the Lord who promised me seventeen years ago that this day would come and I, like Sarah laughed.

The Lord has done great things for us,
and we are filled with joy.
Psalm 126:3

Table of Contents

To Build a

Fill your home with respect... for God, for each other, and for your different personalities.

Make respectful communication the standard. Don't strive to be "right," but rather kind and thoughtful. Gentle corrections, loving honesty, generous praise, and carefully handled conflicts make a home a refuge of peace and safety.

Fill your home often with wonderful sounds, delightful smell and ringing laughter, for they ar the indestructible building blocks of which memories are made.

Healthy Family...

When stress, like an enemy, knocks at your door, disarm him with laughter and playfulness. Laugh at even the most feeble, childish attempt to tell a joke.

Give hugs frequently, especially when they haven't been asked for or are undeserved.

emember truth is not the highest virtue in a family, grace is. Overlook what is not intentional, keep short accounts, freely forgive, and be quick to seek forgiveness when you have wronged or hurt another.

Train children to respect and care for "things" while making sure you communicate they are of greater value than the costliest treasures on earth.

Practice your kindest manners at home with those closest to you. Don't save your finest things to impress strangers, use your treasured china and best linens to celebrate little triumphs along the way.

When disagreements arise, keep to the issue at hand, never use the past as a weapon to win the current battle. Lavish encouragement upon one another. Use your words to build your family, not tear it apart.

Make sure the only "I told you so" ever spoken is "I told you you could do it!"

Turn the television off! Talk to each other. Tell stories. Read a book out loud. Take walks together. Get acquainted. Reminisce about the past. Dream about the future. Pray together.

Interact in a way that brings you face to face, not just side by side.

Slow down... way, way down... and enjoy this moment together. It is priceless and when it is gone, it can never be recaptured.

Audrey Jeanne Roberts

Being a Family is "Olde-Fashioned"

To be a healthy family, you have to be somewhat old-fashioned. Progress may be good in some areas of our lives, but almost all that is "new and exciting" interjects itself between family members, separating us rather than bringing us together.

For example, think of how many times you've sat down to a quiet family evening only to be interrupted by the telephone time and again. Or perhaps someone's pager or cell phone went off. Has "progress" lengthened your work week year by year and now you find you have less time than ever with your family?

Our family struggles, too. Sometimes we have an awful time rounding everybody up for family time. One child has soccer practice and then rushes on to a youth group at church. I have my women's group. Dad has to work late, and a second daughter is an intern for the church junior high group! We think that all of our activities are "good," but they still divide us.

In your family is one family member glued to the television set and another to the computer monitor retrieving email or surfing the net? Has another child spent so much time on the telephone that roots are beginning to grow in her ear? Is it progress to find you have twice as much room in your home as in the house where you grew up, only to find yourself twice as isolated? What price has progress exacted on your family's life?

When I was young there were a lot fewer activities that pulled families apart. There were fewer sports to play and those that were offered were seasonal. When I was growing up, there were significantly fewer extracurricular activities, meetings, and associations. Even at church there were fewer family-dividing activities and more whole-family events. Our family had significantly less money than families have today. We bought fewer clothes and handed them down and down through the entire family (cousins included). We rarely took long or expensive vacations. Instead we took frequent, smaller weekend camping trips in our homely little trailer. But you know what? Less really did mean more! We had more time at home together. We had more time to do yard work and household chores together. More time to read fiction, history, or Bible stories. More time for family meals, potlucks, and neighborhood get-togethers—more time for more family interaction.

When I was growing up, I lived in my grandmother's home for several years. Chatting was the number one favorite activity of Grandmother's household. It seemed that we never ran out of things to talk about, and usually all three generations chattered away together. Cards or game playing followed the chatting, and once in a while on a really special evening Grandmother would tell us stories.

She would tell us all about my grandfather, who had been a pioneer radioman for the Army Air Corp in Alaska. He installed the second radio base ever built in the Alaska territory. First he had to haul the pieces to the site by dog sled, and then he had to build it.

Sometimes rather than talk or play games we would knit, crochet, embroider, sew, or do other handcrafts together. I'll never forget my left-handed grandmother struggling to show me, her right-handed protegé, how to do a cable knit or a fancy crochet stitch. Those times were a priceless, precious heritage. I fear that if I were growing up in her household today, our time would be eaten up by "progress." I would probably be watching the latest video rather than learning lifelong needlework skills at my Grandmother's knee.

Grandmother would tell us stories

There's no way around it, television is here to stay and it has become an enemy to most families. TV tells us daily that "good is evil and evil is good." It assaults us with filthy language, useless information, and sex-inundated plots. It overwhelms us with bad news that we are powerless to change. It leaves us overloaded and paralyzed. But even worse than that, it robs us of positive, family-building activities and time—time that we could have used getting to know each other through the simple pleasures of conversation and sharing. I once told an extended family member that we almost never watch television. She was incredulous and exclaimed: "You don't watch TV? Why, we wouldn't know what to do with each other if we didn't watch television!"

I think it's time for some radical counter assaults against technology's war on our families. Try turning off the television, radio, compact disc player, and any other modern device for one month—perhaps with limited exceptions to stave off a mutiny—and turn the clock back to a time before all these devices became part of our existence. Spend the month doing nothing but old-fashioned activities together. Make a game of it. Think of some of the silly old things you did as a child, like camping out in the backyard. Or play some of the classic board games like Monopoly or Scrabble. Take up a hobby together. Learn how to do a craft. Retrace the steps of a historic family vacation you took when you were a child.

Take up a hobby together

At least make an effort to see which of the modern technological devices is benefiting your family and which is not. Then permanently disconnect those that are driving all of you apart! You know what? Old-fashioned might just be a newfangled way to build your healthy family!

Some More Ideas for Building Healthy Families

What are you actively teaching your children? Do family members discuss daily events together? Do you know what your children think about the world around them? Do they know what you believe? How much time do you spend in face-to-face activities with each other?

Side-by-side activities can be wonderful if they involve training, imparting skills, or giving instruction in areas of interests or hobbies. We try to ask questions of our children regularly (I know, it's tough getting more than a grunt out of them at times!). We ask helpful conversation starters like: "What was the funniest thing that happened at school today?" "Did anything happen that disturbed you today?" "What was the most surprising thing you learned in class today?" "Did things go well with your friends this week, or were there things that were painful or difficult?" Take some time to think up the questions in advance. Then, when you are driving your kids to a doctor's appointment or for a haircut, you will be ready to ask your questions. Then just let them talk.

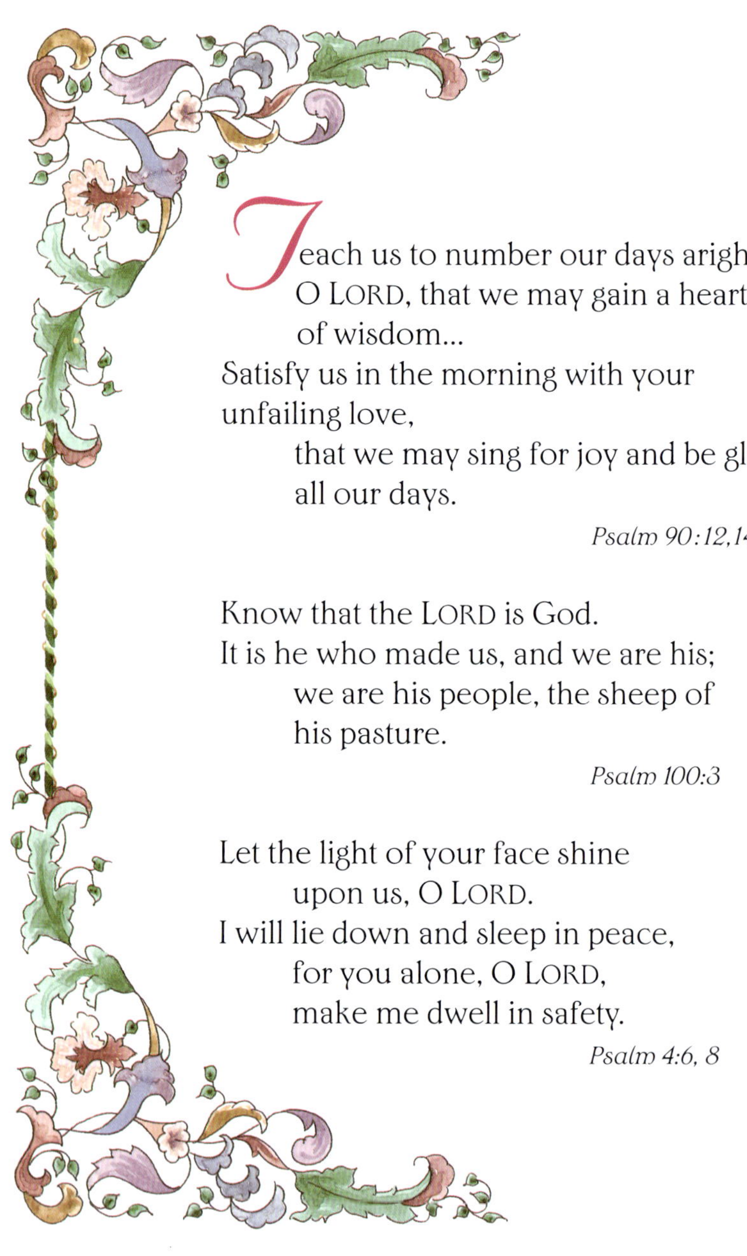

Teach us to number our days aright,
O LORD, that we may gain a heart
of wisdom...
Satisfy us in the morning with your
unfailing love,
that we may sing for joy and be glad
all our days.

Psalm 90:12,14

Know that the LORD is God.
It is he who made us, and we are his;
we are his people, the sheep of
his pasture.

Psalm 100:3

Let the light of your face shine
upon us, O LORD.
I will lie down and sleep in peace,
for you alone, O LORD,
make me dwell in safety.

Psalm 4:6, 8

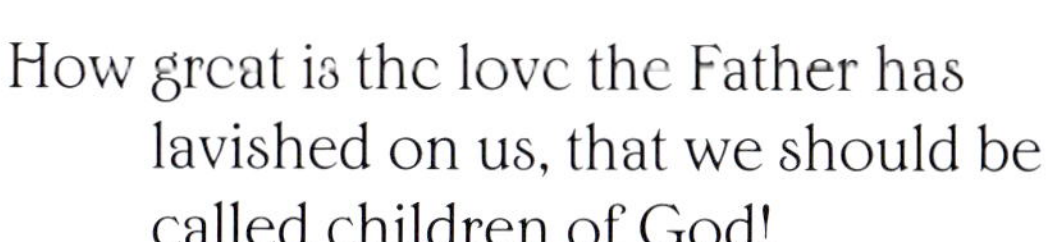

How great is the love the Father has
lavished on us, that we should be
called children of God!

1 John 3:1

Dear friends,

Build yourselves up in your most holy faith and pray in the Holy Spirit. Keep yourselves in God's love as you wait for the mercy of our Lord Jesus Christ to bring you to eternal life.

Jude 20-21

Encourage one another and build each other up.

1 Thessalonians 5:11

Our Family

is like a patchwork quilt,

Of pieces
old and new,

Snips of this
and scraps
of that,

Now aged to
mellow hue.

are stitched together,
helping weather out the storm.
Our friendship, love, commitment
provide comfort to keep us warm.

When
hard
times

come we fear not...
Our stitches stand the test.
For love grows stronger year-by-year,
by God we have been blessed.

Audrey Jeanne Roberts

The Blending of Families

Sometimes families aren't born, they're blended–grafted together. If the graft takes, a new, strong hybrid can begin to grow.

I was the child of a blended family when no one else I knew had a blended family. It was difficult to learn to let someone who was totally new to fathering have the authority role in my life. I didn't "feel" like he was my father, I wasn't sure I even wanted this stranger to be my father. But through marriage to my mother, he was.

He and I struggled, fought, and had many unhappy times. But as the years passed we began to know each other. We began to be a family. When my maternal grandmother had a debilitating stroke and was completely helpless, my parents uprooted their own lives and went to San Diego to take care of her so she wouldn't have to be placed in a nursing home. I watched my stepfather lovingly, carefully tend to my grandmother at all hours of the day and night. Grandmother hadn't even been kind to him, yet he loved her with the love of Christ. It was during this time that I came to respect and love my stepfather as my father.

When my first husband was dying, he often told me he wanted me to remarry. I was more than reluctant. I knew I didn't want my home to be the battleground that my childhood home had been. I decided that I would simply wait to remarry until my children were grown. Then if God had someone for me, I'd consider it. But as usual, God had other plans!

The joys of a blended family

When Steve and I met and eventually married, God began to show us the joys of a blended family. He walked us step by step through the bonding process, and we learned many valuable lessons along the way.

We learned that feelings follow decisions. I decided to love Steve's children, Scot and Ariane, because God gave them to me to love. It was that simple! But I didn't feel like their mother. I didn't have any sweet early memories of their childhood to recall. They sprang into my life almost fully grown and mature. But once I accepted my assignment from God and chose to love them, the feelings inevitably followed. My feelings for Scot and Ariane are different than what I feel for my natural-born daughters. But they are as real as the love I have for my own children by birth.

Sometimes in a blended family it can be hard to

understand one another because we don't share genetic traits and family histories. I can look at my children by birth and think, "Oh, she's acting just like my sister," or "That's her dad all over again." We get used to certain traits that run in our family and we've learned ways to work around or with them. But in a blended family, we encounter completely different personalities, perspectives, and tendencies. Those in a blended family need to give themselves time to understand one another—to learn each other's ways and personalities. They need time to work through differences and embrace rather than resent them.

Work through differences and embrace them

We learned that choosing to embrace the new family doesn't mean replacing or devaluing the old. The new family is different—not necessarily better or worse, just different. One of my late husband's last instructions to me was this, "Please tell my girls that I would never consider it a betrayal of their love for me if they come to love another man as father." As the adults, we need to lead our children and give them permission to love another party, to welcome that person to the family. The greatest destruction in stepfamilies occurs when there is a tug of war for the children's affections.

The hardest things about blended families are accepting each other's limitations and being careful about our expectations. I can never act like Ariane's mother would act, we are two uniquely different individuals, I can't see the world from her mother's perspective, I can't respond to Ariane as she would. I can't even guess how she would respond because I don't know her. But I can be me. I can bring value to Ariane by bringing different perspectives and different strengths into her life—perspectives and strengths to which she would not otherwise be exposed.

We need to give ourselves time. Time to adjust, time to heal, time to grow together, and time to make our own memories. All of life, all of its history and tradition, has changed for both of our families.

We have a choice. We can cling to the old or we can forge a new future incorporating the best of the old and some uniquely new things that belong just to this new blended family. As a step-parent, I've discovered that I need to draw out the things that meant the most to the children from their former family and if appropriate be willing to incorporate them into our new family's traditions. In most blended family situations it will take five years or more for the new

We can forge a new future

family to become established and comfortable. Give yourself and your children the time and the freedom to grow into a new family, and you may find that God has truly "worked all things together for good," bringing his wonderful redemptive power to the pain of the past.

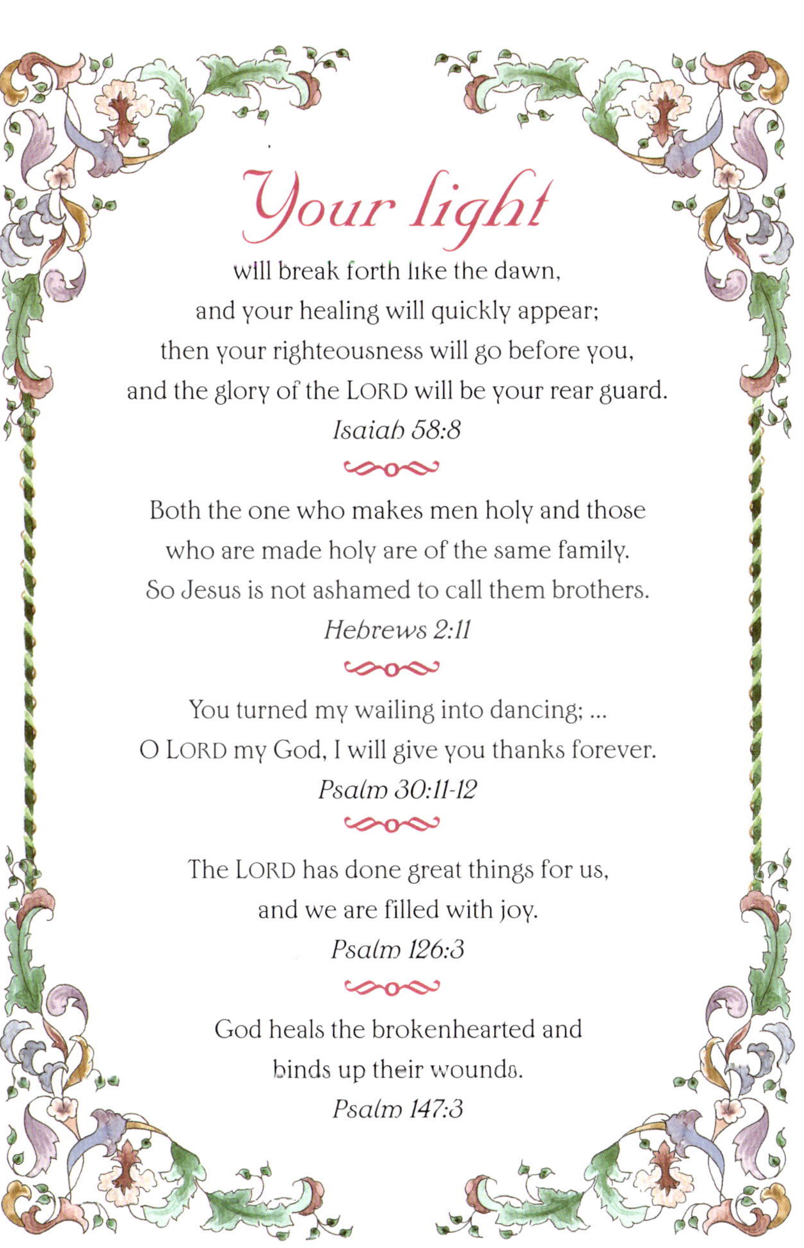

Your light

will break forth like the dawn,
and your healing will quickly appear;
then your righteousness will go before you,
and the glory of the LORD will be your rear guard.

Isaiah 58:8

Both the one who makes men holy and those
who are made holy are of the same family.
So Jesus is not ashamed to call them brothers.

Hebrews 2:11

You turned my wailing into dancing; ...
O LORD my God, I will give you thanks forever.

Psalm 30:11-12

The LORD has done great things for us,
and we are filled with joy.

Psalm 126:3

God heals the brokenhearted and
binds up their wounds.

Psalm 147:3

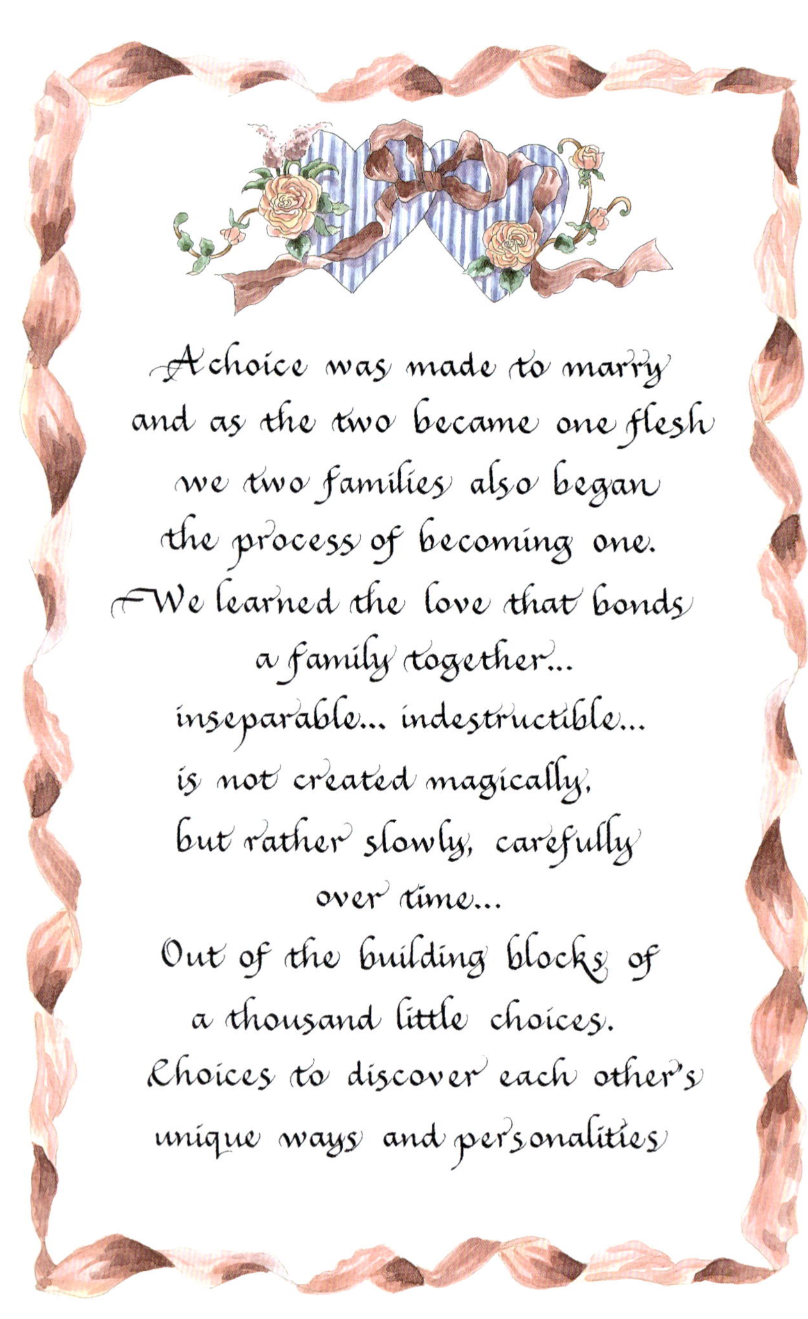

A choice was made to marry
and as the two became one flesh
we two families also began
the process of becoming one.
We learned the love that bonds
a family together...
inseparable... indestructible...
is not created magically,
but rather slowly, carefully
over time...
Out of the building blocks of
a thousand little choices.
Choices to discover each other's
unique ways and personalities

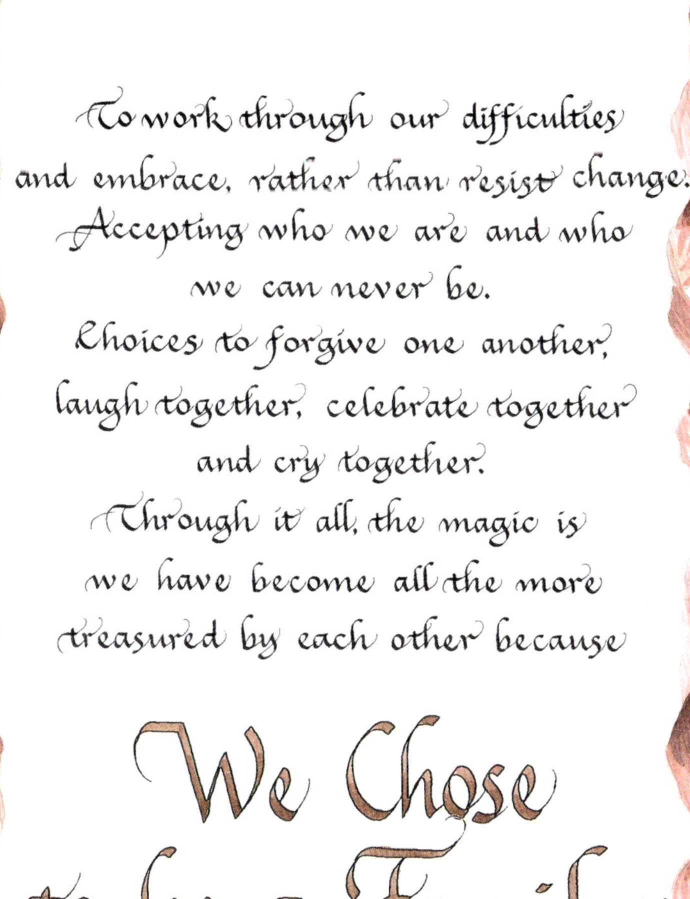

Audrey Jeanne Roberts

Family Traditions

The Glue that Binds Generations as One

"Family traditions." Those two words have the power to conjure up sights, sounds, smells, and memories. The essence of tradition hangs in the air like a fragrant perfume long after the event that created it has faded into the past. We anticipate a season or holiday festivity because of the traditions it holds. Traditions stir our emotions. They bring precious people to life again in our hearts and minds as we continue to enjoy the traditions they began. Traditions are the links that hook one generation to the next, much as the links in a chain join a collection of many jewels to form a dazzling necklace.

What is a tradition? It can be anything your family enjoys enough to do again and again. Traditions can be permanent or temporary. They can last through many lifetimes or span just a few years. Your family's traditions will be very different than my family's. Your traditions will be utterly unique and special to you. Traditions don't have to be old to be special. New ones are fun too. God loves traditions, especially those that draw our hearts toward him and those that help us remember his goodness towards us.

Our family surely has one of the most bizarre Christmas traditions ever. In December of 1994, Steve and I were preparing to be married on New Year's Eve. We had been working hard to create our own wedding vows, and we were talking about them as we did some last minute Christmas shopping (as in the last minute before the stores closed on Christmas Eve!).

We walked into a department store and saw an older gentleman and his wife just ahead of us. He was wearing the most intensely lemon yellow plaid pants and a matching lemon yellow golf shirt. I turned to Steve and said, "Honey, I love you, but I don't think I could vow to 'Love, honor, and walk beside you no matter what you wear!'"

Traditions stir our emotions

We had a good laugh and then went on with our shopping. Toward the end of the day we stopped in a card shop and I bought Steve the perfect Christmas card. It was a black, tuxedo-shaped card with a bright red cummerbund and tie. Inside it rambled on about how lucky I was to have a husband who was so elegant and handsome. I grabbed it because it was so incredibly true.

The next morning, after literally staying up all night wrapping presents, our soon-to-be blended families prepared to spend our first Christmas together. Steve disappeared upstairs for the longest time and we were growing restless to proceed. Then to our amazement, he came parading down the stairs like a proud peacock in all his finery. He was wearing red tartan, semi bell-bottom pants, a red shirt with a plaid collar, a paisley tie, and a multi-colored plaid hat. He strutted into the room and asked me, "Would you walk beside me in this outfit." We all laughed so hard we cried. Then I showed him my tuxedo card and we laughed some more.

Later on after opening presents, my oldest daughter, Jennifer, who was thirteen years old, picked up her new Chicago Bulls jacket and held it up with the arms spread wide. "The power of the Bull over the power of the plaid," she shouted at Steve. He chased her all over the house trying to rub some plaid on her to make her cool. The fun continued when we went to visit the neighbors later in the morning with Steve proudly wearing his plaid and me walking beside him—wherever he went!

Some traditions are for a season

From this inauspicious beginning, the children began to plot their outfits for next year's Christmas morning. They decided to establish a contest for the most outrageous costume. We sang Christmas carols for our neighbors the next few Christmas mornings in the most un-Christmas-like outfits you could imagine. This tradition continued until we left that neighborhood. Remember that I said that some traditions are for a season and some are for a lifetime? Well, we didn't quite think this particular tradition would move very well, so we let it go. It had served its purpose. It had helped make one family out of two. It had broken the ice of our first Christmas together and given us something unique to look forward to in the next. Such is the role of traditions.

Creating Traditions

Most traditions just happen. We do something and enjoy it so much we want to do it over and over again. We travel to a special summer vacation spot. We see a certain special performance at Christmas or Easter. We go to visit Grandma or another special relative. When you are looking for something to do this year, think back to the past few years. What bears repeating? Pencil it into the schedule and make it a tradition.

Special foods make for great traditions. You can smell their fragrance, your mouth waters just thinking of them. The shared activity of preparing them—as in baking cookies and pies—makes them special as well. Plan time to prepare the foods that are rich in your cultural or familial tradition. Don't prepare them alone and feel like a slave in the galley. Invite others to join in and make the tradition even richer.

Music can bring back memories as powerfully as sights and smells. Small investments in unique and wonderful music will create a festive and memorable ambiance. Bring out the old CDs, tapes, and records year after year and they will become a dynamic tradition.

Decorations don't have to be expensive. In fact they can be simple items that touch our emotions and make those around us feel cared for and remembered. For every birthday celebration, we decorate our dining room chandelier with something that reflects the interests or joys of the individual we're honoring. My "plaid man's" birthday was celebrated this year with every plaid item we could find. Plaid candles, plaid cloth napkins tied together like a garland strung across the entrance to the dining room, plaid ribbon, and on and on it went!

Think back to your childhood. What was special to you? Did the tradition have enough value to you and your family to continue doing it with the next generation? My grandmother bought us a Lifesavers holiday book of candy every Christmas. When I buy my own children their books of Lifesavers, it brings Grandmother back to my holidays, even though she's been gone for years. I buy a special candy orange that peels apart in sections for my stepdaughter. It's a tradition from her early years that means Christmas to her, so I keep it alive to remind her of her past while we forge a future together.

Your Turn

Traditions we've had:

Traditions I'd like to start:

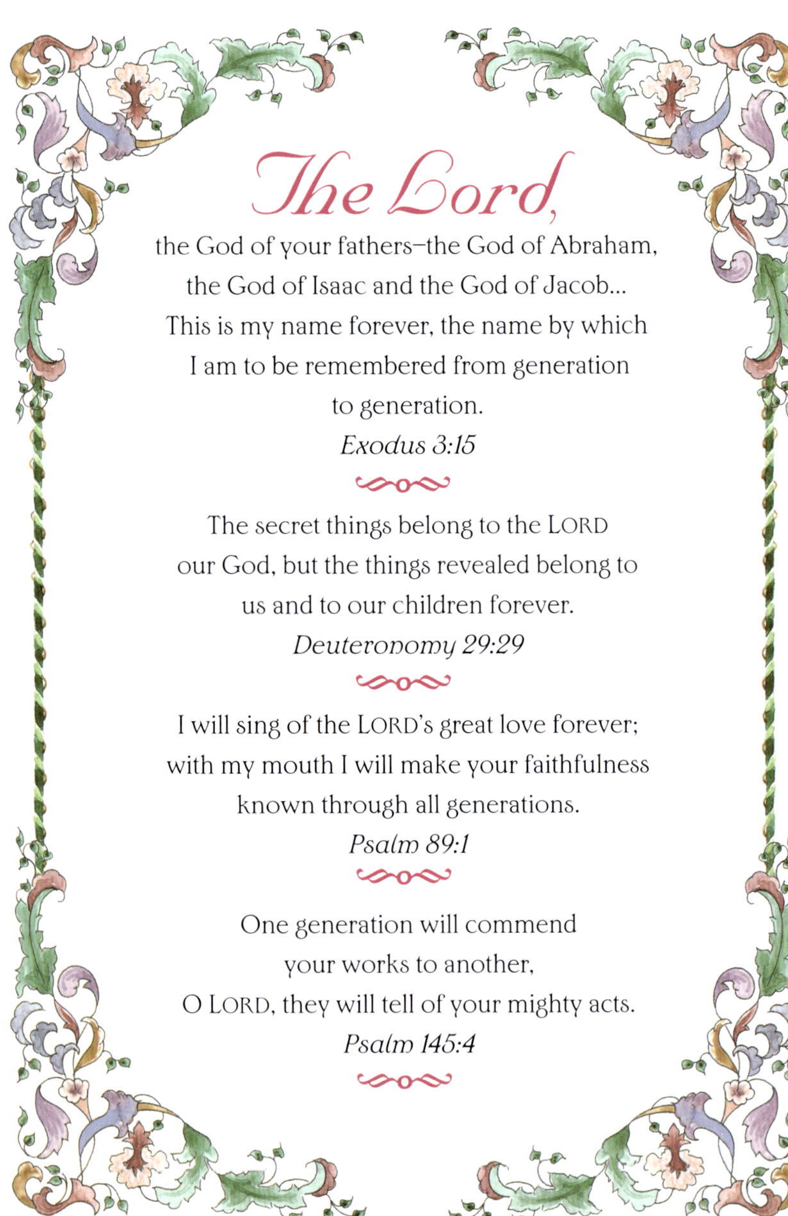

The Lord,

the God of your fathers—the God of Abraham,
the God of Isaac and the God of Jacob...
This is my name forever, the name by which
I am to be remembered from generation
to generation.

Exodus 3:15

The secret things belong to the LORD
our God, but the things revealed belong to
us and to our children forever.

Deuteronomy 29:29

I will sing of the LORD's great love forever;
with my mouth I will make your faithfulness
known through all generations.

Psalm 89:1

One generation will commend
your works to another,
O LORD, they will tell of your mighty acts.

Psalm 145:4

Our Family

No nuclear family ever lives in true isolation. There are those who have gone before us, those who will follow after us, and those who live life with us. God has created powerful links to help us forge a family chain of strength and substance. Some of these links are physical—genetic similarities that show we are the product of our parents' oneness. But many of our links to our family members are spiritual.

My family on my father's side is rather large by today's standards. He had five sisters and each of them had at least two or more children. Unfortunately, when I was eight years old I was separated from this side of my family by my parents' divorce. When I attended my Aunt Susie's wedding in September of 1978, I hadn't seen any of the family in twelve years.

My Aunt Susie is only a year older than I am. Susie and I had great fun as children. We loved to confuse our friends and neighbors with our aunt/niece relationship. We had been very close in my early years, but now I was somewhat nervous about seeing relatives that I no longer really knew. Would we have anything in common anymore? Would they accept me? Would I fit into the well-established structure of this closely-knit family?

These were my thoughts as I flew to Portland, Oregon. Dad brought my grandparents along to meet me at the airport. I had only seen them briefly two other times during all those years. But now it was as if no time had passed since I'd last seen them. We talked about everything well into the night.

The next day was the rehearsal for Susie and Craig's wedding. When we arrived at the church, everyone but me had roles to play and things to do, so I simply sat in the middle of a pew in the center of the church and watched the proceedings. I can see now that I selected my seating as a physical expression of my internal sense of isolation, of being an outsider.

Suddenly, someone I didn't recognize came up to me and asked me a question I couldn't begin to answer. The blank look in my eyes stopped her short. "Oh! You're not Becky! I thought you were Becky! You look just like her! Who are you?" Becky was another of my aunts who was only five years older than I.

"I'm Audrey, Keith's daughter..." I got no further. I was instantly embraced in an excited, enveloping hug and my re-entry into this side of my family began. There was much excitement as she dragged me off by the hand to introduce me to the rest of my cousins, "Audrey's here and doesn't she look just like Becky?" All through the rehearsal, the wedding, and the reception, this scene was repeated over and over again. "You look like Becky" from one "You sound like Becky" from another.

At that wedding, we witnessed the powerful genetic link that the Lord has built into us. Though separated by a thousand miles and twelve years, we are so similar in personality, characteristics, and mannerisms as well as appearance that you would think Becky and I were twins. Because Becky and I are close in age, we have been blessed to see more clearly the strength of a family's physical connectedness.

The heritage of a shared family faith

When we look at our living family tree, the branches that form the canopy are of shelter and love. Entwined there are traces and hints of those who have gone before us. My grandparents are able to see traces of family ancestors in their grandchildren and great-grandchildren. We have talents, traits, and gifts that have passed from generation to generation. These must be bittersweet remembrances of long-lost loved ones, that stir in their minds as they watch us develop.

There is a second and even more powerful link that our Father gives to connect us as one. It is the heritage of a shared family faith and the bond that results after years of praying for each other. We often marvel at how wonderfully intact our father's side of the family has remained. It seems we have been unusually blessed with very few divorces or even deaths. The only explanation appears to be that my grandparents' lifelong commitment to each other and to their offspring has been manifested in their daily prayers for every single member of their beloved clan.

My grandfather has a wall he calls his "Rogue's Gallery." It is packed with a conglomeration of matted and framed photo collages–the frozen moments of our family's history–weddings, showers, graduations, school photographs, and a host of informal family gatherings. Grandpa surveys this gallery each night before retiring and intercedes on our behalf. God has honored my grandparents love for him and for those he has entrusted to them.

My grandparents are simple people who were determined to raise their children in a Christian home, though neither of them came from one. They were faithful to each other, to their children, and to the churches they attended. They taught Sunday school at times, led Bible studies, and rendered whatever service the Lord required of them in a quiet, consistent manner.

And what has been the result of this simple faithfulness? Though many in the family have wandered far from the faith, most have returned to it later in life. Though most members of the family have faced their share of hardships and challenges, every child, grandchild, and great-grandchild knows the Lord. The family includes pastors, leaders, and teachers whom God has raised up to minister in the local church just as my grandparents did. The children that have sprung up from my grandparent's union have been faithful to the Lord and to his calling, however great or small that calling might be.

Lift your family up

No matter how far or near to the Lord your family is today, you can pray. You can lift your family up to heaven and seek the Lord's blessing upon their lives.

Lord,

Give me the faith to be the foundation for a spiritual heritage that will follow long after I am gone. Give me eyes to see what you want to do in each life and even in the lives yet to come—those that I may never get to see here on this earth.

Remind me Lord, when I get too busy with the cares of this life, that you have called me to a great and wonderful role, that of building a strong and healthy family committed and equipped to do your work here on the earth!

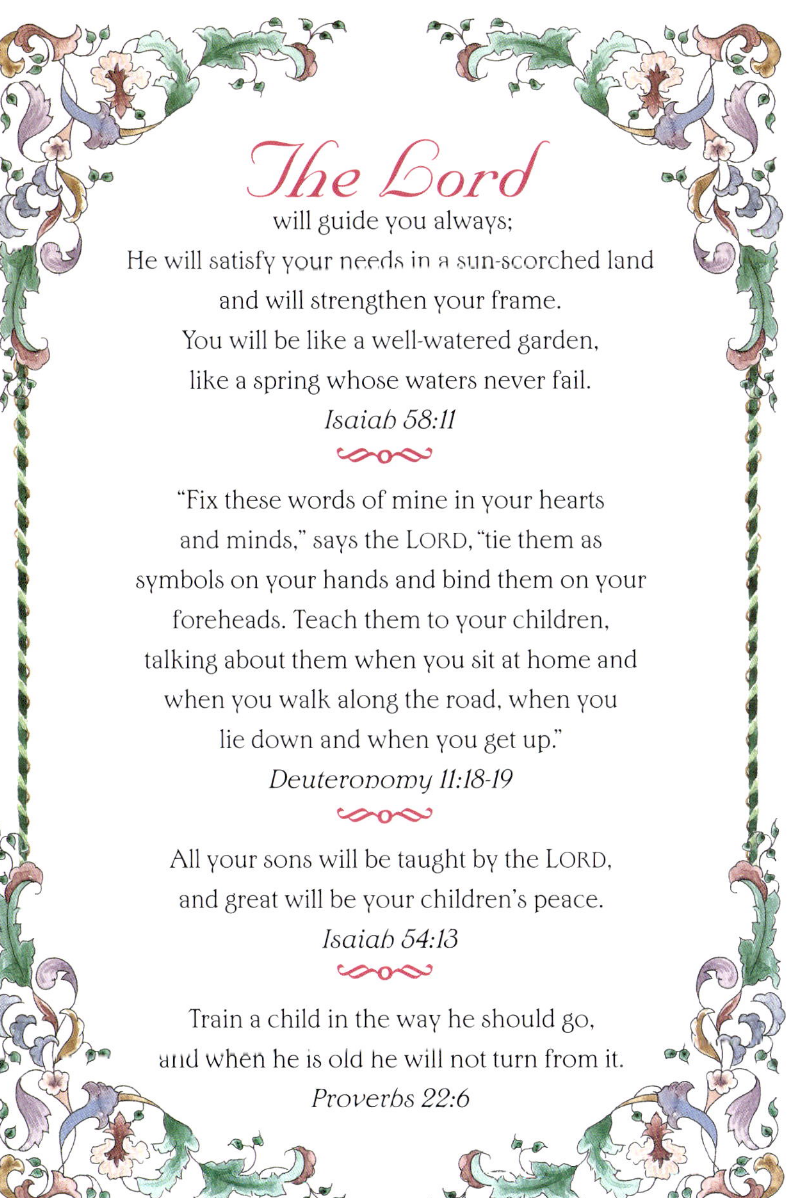

The Lord

will guide you always;
He will satisfy your needs in a sun-scorched land
and will strengthen your frame.
You will be like a well-watered garden,
like a spring whose waters never fail.

Isaiah 58:11

"Fix these words of mine in your hearts and minds," says the LORD, "tie them as symbols on your hands and bind them on your foreheads. Teach them to your children, talking about them when you sit at home and when you walk along the road, when you lie down and when you get up."

Deuteronomy 11:18-19

All your sons will be taught by the LORD,
and great will be your children's peace.

Isaiah 54:13

Train a child in the way he should go,
and when he is old he will not turn from it.

Proverbs 22:6

A Fruitful Family

My husband says that apart from one notable exception, I'm pretty easy to live with. He tells our friends "She has PMS–*Post Midnight Syndrome*, and I've learned to send her to bed at the stroke of twelve or suffer the consequences!"

When we are on the road doing trade shows, it's not unusual for us to work sixteen hours straight, side-by-side. Recently, near the end of such a day, around midnight, a fellow exhibitor with whom we had previously shared our faith came over to speak with me.

"I've been watching you two. You are so kind to one another. You have to be as stressed out and exhausted as the rest of us, and yet you're still so peaceful. It's obvious you really like one another. You either put on a very good act in public (and I don't think that's the case) or you're really living out your faith. I think it's the latter, and that there's something about your faith that is worth investigating."

What she didn't know was at that very moment I had been wrestling with my feelings of frustration, exhaustion, and irritation but had chosen to remain quiet. The Lord had been whispering to my heart, *"Is this worth being unkind over? How important is it to be right? Isn't it more important to be kind?"* My faith had been "on stage" during my struggle and I didn't even know it!

The fruit of the Spirit is one of the evidences of our faith that is visible to the world. When we invited the Lord into our lives, he gave us a new nature, his nature. His Spirit takes up residence in us. We need his nature to produce his fruit in the same way only a tended and watered orange tree can produce good oranges. You can't be good enough or work hard enough to produce fruit on your own.

My faith had been "on stage"

In my orange grove, it is my responsibility as the gardener to give the trees water and fertilizer. With nourishment from me, my trees more or less rest in the sunshine and grow. They don't break into a sweat or strive to be fruitful. They produce fruit because it is natural for them when they are well cared for. In the same way, the Lord is my husbandman and he develops his fruit in my life. He is my Living Water and Bread of Life (John 6:35 and John 7:38). He nourishes me each day with his love and guidance. With that kind of care, I can't help but produce good fruit.

Before the oranges can be sent abroad, they must be

home-grown and then harvested. That is also a perfect picture of what God wants me to do. First he wants me to produce abundant fruit at home and then send it abroad. The Lord helped me to cultivate a kind and loving relationship with my husband at home. In turn, that fruit was "sent abroad" when we displayed that love and kindness outside of our home in a stressful situation.

Our pastor's wife recently paid him one of the highest public tributes a man can receive. She stood in front of a large gathering of couples at our Valentine's Day Dinner and said, "The man you hear every Sunday morning, the man you see standing in the pulpit and think you know, is exactly the same man I'm married to at home. He lives the things he preaches and teaches." Wow! I want to hear my husband, children, and friends say the same thing about me!

There's a powerful message to my heart here. Home is where bearing the fruit of the Spirit starts and counts the most. If the world praises me as writer and an artist, or says that I'm intelligent, witty, and brilliant, but my children say that I am unkind, mean, and bitter, none of what I do matters. My heart is not being fruitful where it really counts. My highest goal is to be Christ-like and to bear fruit, at home first (where it can sometimes be the most challenging), and then in the world.

Therefore

as God's chosen people, holy and dearly loved, clothe yourselves with compassion, kindness, humility, gentleness and patience. Bear with each other and forgive whatever grievances you may have against one another. Forgive as the Lord forgave you. And over all these virtues put on love, which binds them all together in perfect unity.

Colossians 3:12-14

The fruit of the Spirit is love, joy, peace, patience, kindness, goodness, faithfulness, gentleness and self-control. Since we live by the Spirit, let us keep in step with the Spirit.

Galatians 5:22-23, 25

Jesus said, "Remain in me, and I will remain in you. No branch can bear fruit by itself; it must remain in the vine. Neither can you bear fruit unless you remain in me."

John 15:4

Be kind and compassionate to one another, forgiving each other, just as in Christ God forgave you.

Ephesians 4:32

Our Home
... may

it be a place of peace

joy and quietness of heart,
a refuge and sanctuary in
times of need.

May there be encouragement
for the weary,
Strength for the weak,
And love in unbounded measure

for family & friend alike

Audrey Jeanne Roberts

I was eight when my mother divorced and had to return to school full-time to get her teaching degree. It was one of the only acceptable professions a woman of her day could pursue and earn an adequate living for her family. For her those were long, exhausting days filled with studying and the stress of living once again in my grandmother's home. Mother's schedule didn't leave her much emotional energy to invest in us children. We just didn't get many hugs growing up in our household.

After wandering away from the Lord, I turned back to him in my early twenties. I found myself attending a newly-founded, warmly-affectionate church that was great—except that people in the church had the annoying habit of hugging each other—a lot.

I had grown up in a conservative Baptist church where a firm handshake was just about the extent of physical displays of emotion. I wasn't comfortable with hugging in church or anywhere else for that matter, so Sunday mornings became a cat-and-mouse game for me. There was this greeter at the door, a small, older gentleman who was so full of the love of the Lord that he felt it was his calling to hug every person who came through the door on Sunday morning. I was so uncomfortable with the thought of hugging a stranger that I would wait outside and time my entrance to the exact moment he was engaged in greeting some other person. Then I could quickly slip by!

Once I mistimed my entrance. Blushing, I bent over, and attempted to give him a quick, obligatory hug. Instead I found myself staring into his love-filled eyes and hearing him say, "Jesus loves you so much—and I do too! Welcome sister." Then he enveloped me in a hug that made me feel like Jesus had reached out and touched me personally. I blushed again, stammered something unintelligible in response, and rushed to my seat. Then, as if my entrance wasn't difficult enough, the pastor had us turn to one another in a time of fellowship and introduce ourselves by shaking hands or hugging. I cannot adequately describe how uncomfortable and squeamish it made me to face those times in church.

I wasn't comfortable with hugging

One Sunday morning I realized that the Lord wanted to change my heart about physical displays of affection. He wanted to help me become comfortable connecting to other Christians and family members through the gift of hugging. I prayed, "Lord, for some reason I am really, really uncomfortable with this whole idea of hugging. Please change my heart. Help me become comfortable expressing my love through a hug."

God answered that prayer with a vengeance! He gave me a wonderful freedom to hug others—family, friends, and acquaintances. He melted my fearful, isolated heart and helped me not only break the cycle of emotional distance as I raised my own family, but to reach out to my mother and grandmother and physically demonstrate my love for them as well. We began to hug in our family, at first awkwardly and timidly, but now it is with the freedom of those who love one another and are not afraid to express it openly.

A hug says "I love you"

A hug says "I love you," "I accept you," and "You're valuable to me." A hug can console grief or encourage the discouraged heart like nothing else can. Hugs allow us to connect with one another, to empathize with each other, and to share the joys of life with one another. Our days become a little healthier and a little happier when we fill them with hugs!

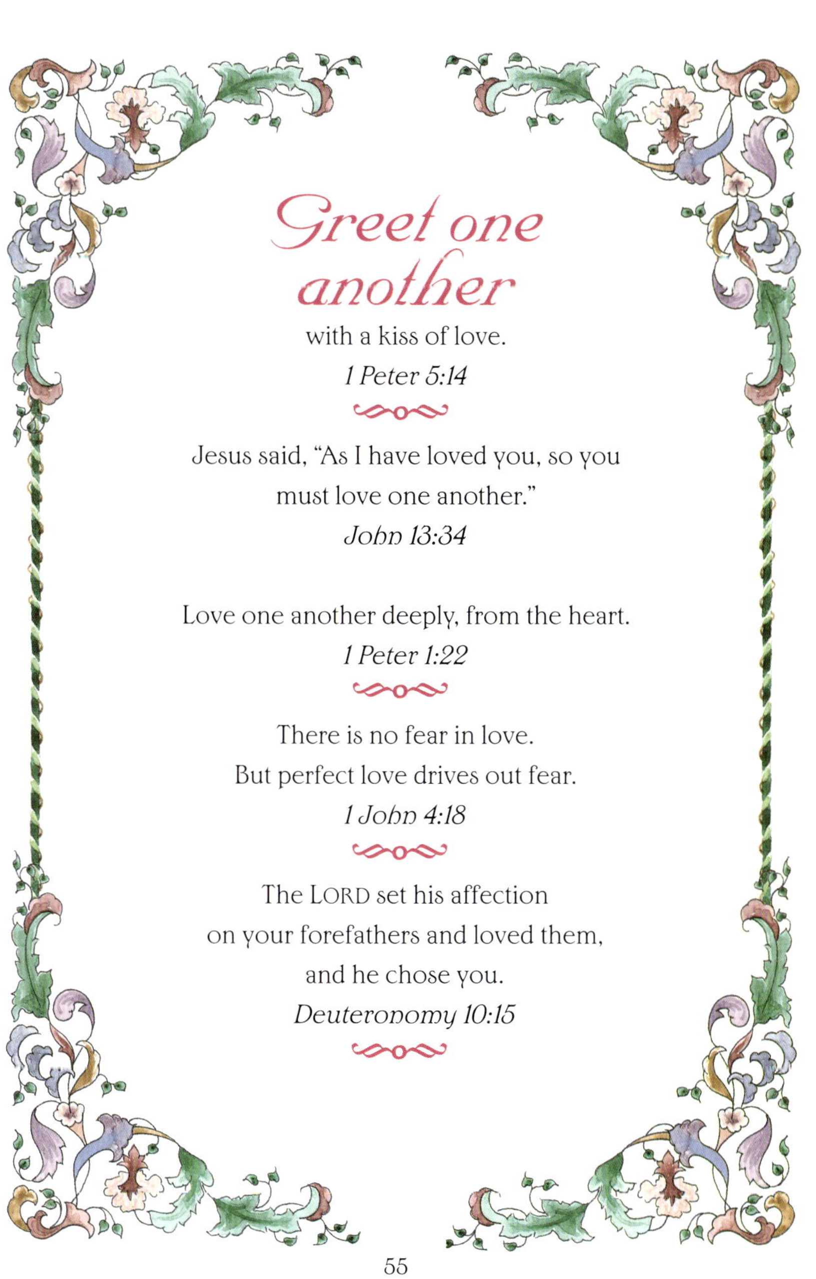

Greet one another

with a kiss of love.

1 Peter 5:14

Jesus said, "As I have loved you, so you
must love one another."

John 13:34

Love one another deeply, from the heart.

1 Peter 1:22

There is no fear in love.
But perfect love drives out fear.

1 John 4:18

The LORD set his affection
on your forefathers and loved them,
and he chose you.

Deuteronomy 10:15

Hugs are the perfect gift
They work for people of
all ages, sizes, & shapes.
They can be given to family
and friends alike.
You can never have
too many of them.
They are good for your heart,
are non-fattening,
extremely affordable
and one-size-fits-all!
A hug a day
keeps the blues away.

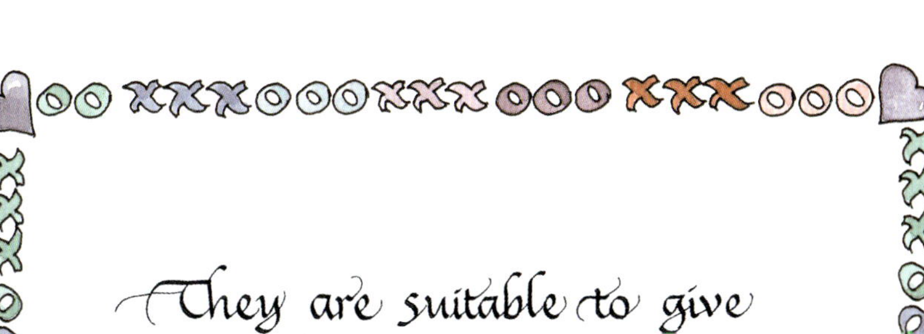

They are suitable to give
for any occasion,
but often are considered
most valuable when
given for no occasion at all.
They are a gift that brings
as much joy to the giver
as the recipient
and the giver of a hug
will never resent it
when it is returned!

Audrey Jeanne Roberts

Laughter

If you scroll down through the most treasured memories of your childhood, chances are many of them will be accompanied by a "laugh track." Healthy families laugh together—a lot! Healthy families learn to laugh rather than scream in frustration. They learn the fine art of disciplining with humor instead of anger. In families, a great sense of humor is like the oil in a motor. It reduces friction and protects against excess wear and tear.

Our favorite comedian, Bill Cosby, has provided our family with countless hours of laughter. We've memorized almost every line he's ever had to say about children, families, and parenting. He's so right about our family life that we're sure he's been watching us. Some days Bill has helped us hold on to what little sanity we have left.

Laughter starts early in the life of a child. If you've been privileged to raise a child from babyhood, you will immediately recall the sound of the infinitely precious, deep belly laughs of an infant. It rumbles up from their toes and often leaves them gasping for air with fits of hiccups! Somewhere in the early months of life, your child discovered the gift of laughter and then spread laughter throughout the entire household.

When I think of laughter in our home, I think of Dad and his kids rolling around on the floor wrestling with each other (inevitably, just before bedtime) producing shrieks and howls of laughter. Or I think of my first grader making a first attempt at telling a joke while doubled over with a case of the giggles. I think of my youngest daughter at age twelve, suddenly, out of nowhere developing a full-blown, virtually adult sense of the absurd.

Healthy families laugh together

One evening not long ago, one of my employees and her new beau came by the house to share dinner with us. Somehow in the course of the evening the conversation degenerated into a sharing contest of "The stupidest thing you ever did as a child and survived to tell." Story after story came out. We were amazed at God's protection and wondered how the angels survived protecting us to adulthood! We laughed literally for hours! We laughed so hard our sides ached and then we laughed because our laughter was so funny!

Laughter is exhausting. Laughter is refreshing. The stress seems to drain out of our minds and hearts and bodies as we laugh together. Somehow laughter helps to recharge our batteries and acts like a medicine for our bones.

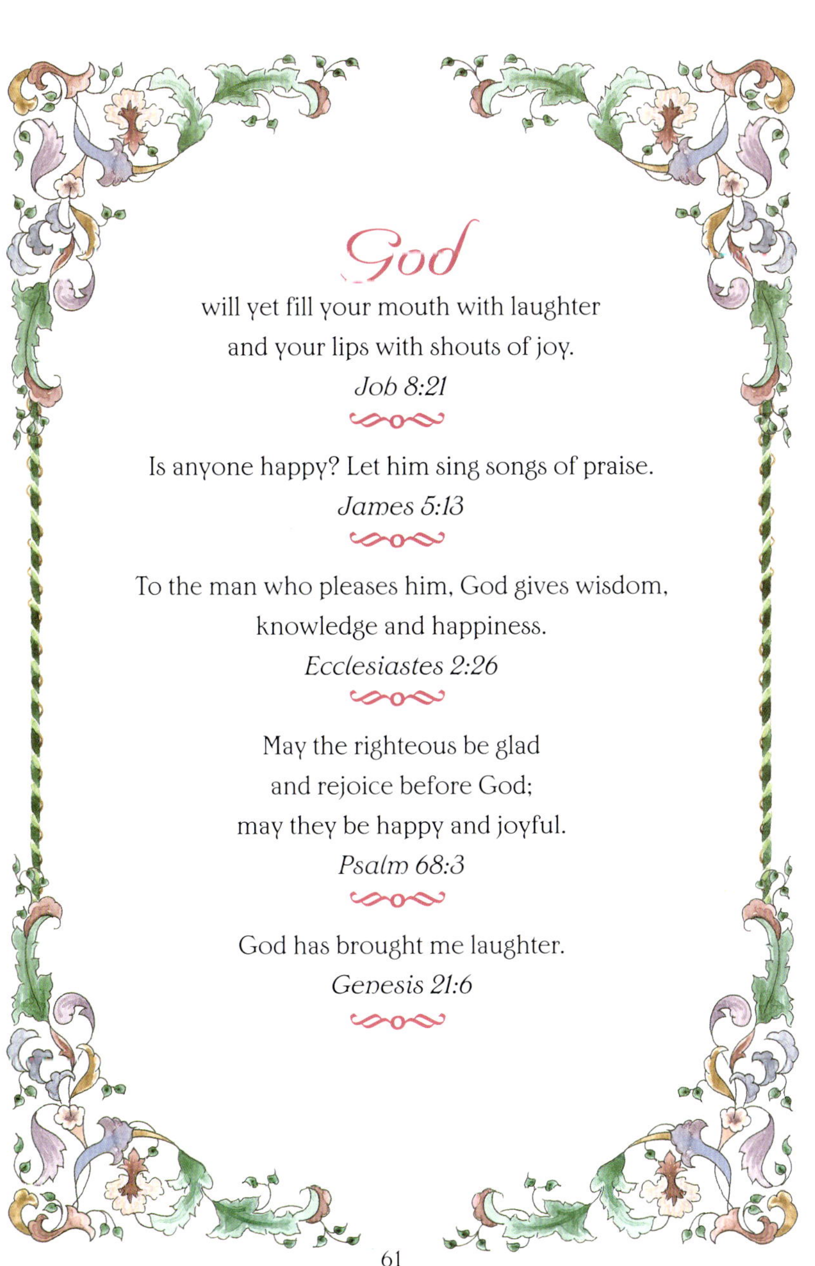

God

will yet fill your mouth with laughter
and your lips with shouts of joy.

Job 8:21

Is anyone happy? Let him sing songs of praise.

James 5:13

To the man who pleases him, God gives wisdom,
knowledge and happiness.

Ecclesiastes 2:26

May the righteous be glad
and rejoice before God;
may they be happy and joyful.

Psalm 68:3

God has brought me laughter.

Genesis 21:6

Family Worship

For those families that share the bond of Christ as the center of their home, family worship is one of the greatest privileges available on this earth. There is incredible power available to the family that embraces its faith in real and practical ways at home. Often when we hear a message about family devotions, our first response is one of overwhelming guilt. We feel inadequate. In all honesty, we have to admit that although we plan to do family devotions in a structured weekly format, we will more than likely begin but not continue them. So then we either begin anticipating failure, or we don't begin at all so that we won't fail! The Lord has not called us to bondage, but to freedom. He desires us to have a light and easy yoke, not a heavy burden!

One of the ways God has helped our family worship and spiritual growth is through spontaneity. When our children tell us about friends who are facing hard times, our response will always be, "Let's take a moment and pray about this right now." We stop immediately, take a few minutes, and ask God to help these people.

At times we play a new worship CD full blast in our home and simply sing and share the music together! Other times we read books together. We've enjoyed reading through *The Chronicles of Narnia* twice, and we've read Frank Peretti's wonderful books *This Present Darkness* and *Piercing the Darkness* as well.

At other times, God uses our circumstances to teach us the lessons he wants us to learn. I am studying the book *Experiencing God* with my Wednesday night women's group. Some time ago, I felt in my heart that my husband and I needed to do my homework lesson for the class together. Every time I walked by the book in my office, the same thought was impressed upon my heart. It took me two days to finally respond!

Play a new worship CD

At that time our company was facing a difficult financial dry spell and we were quite concerned about our cash flow. The lesson in *Experiencing God* that the Lord had shown me that we should study together just happened to be all about faith and finances!

As we read together, our two girls casually came into the living room and invited themselves to participate. So we ended up walking through the lesson together as a family. That evening was one of those sessions of pure honesty and open communication. We sought the Lord together as a family. My husband voiced his heart to the Lord, "Lord, it sure would be nice for once if someone just called and said, 'I was praying for you and I thought I would call and ask if you needed some money right now.' Lord, you know that we've been obedient to meet others' needs this way in the past and now it would be nice if you'd speak to someone about meeting our needs." We talked then about some of the times when we had been a part of the miracle of meeting others' needs anonymously and how wonderful it was to be used by God in this way.

Believe it or not just ten minutes later, even before we'd ended family worship time, the phone rang. A relative was calling to discuss a family matter that led to my being honest about our financial situation. She asked, "Could you use some money right now?"

We sought the Lord together

The conversation ultimately led her to wire a significant sum of money to us the very next day! She had it available to loan and God led her to make the offer in such a dramatic way that all of our hearts were greatly encouraged in faith.

These spontaneous, Spirit-led moments that are inspired by the Lord and embraced by our family have built us up, brick by brick, layer upon layer until we have developed a rich heritage of shared experience in the Lord.

I once read a short story in a magazine about a single mother whose son wanted to pray for a red kite. She had no money and was afraid that if she let her son pray so specifically, he might be disappointed if God didn't answer his prayers. But she nervously led her son in a time of prayer for a beautiful red kite. Within days, a windstorm kicked up and one morning shortly after the storm, the son came running into his mother's room. "God answered my prayers! God gave me a red kite!" He took his mother's hand and pulled her to the front yard to see his new red kite gently dangling in a tree. They easily untangled it and brought it into the house. The kite had not a single rip or tear, just a broken thread at the end where it had torn loose. This mother realized how perfectly trustworthy God was with her son's tender young faith.

We can trust God with our needs and we can trust him with the process of building us up as a family into the character, nature, and faith of our Lord Jesus Christ.

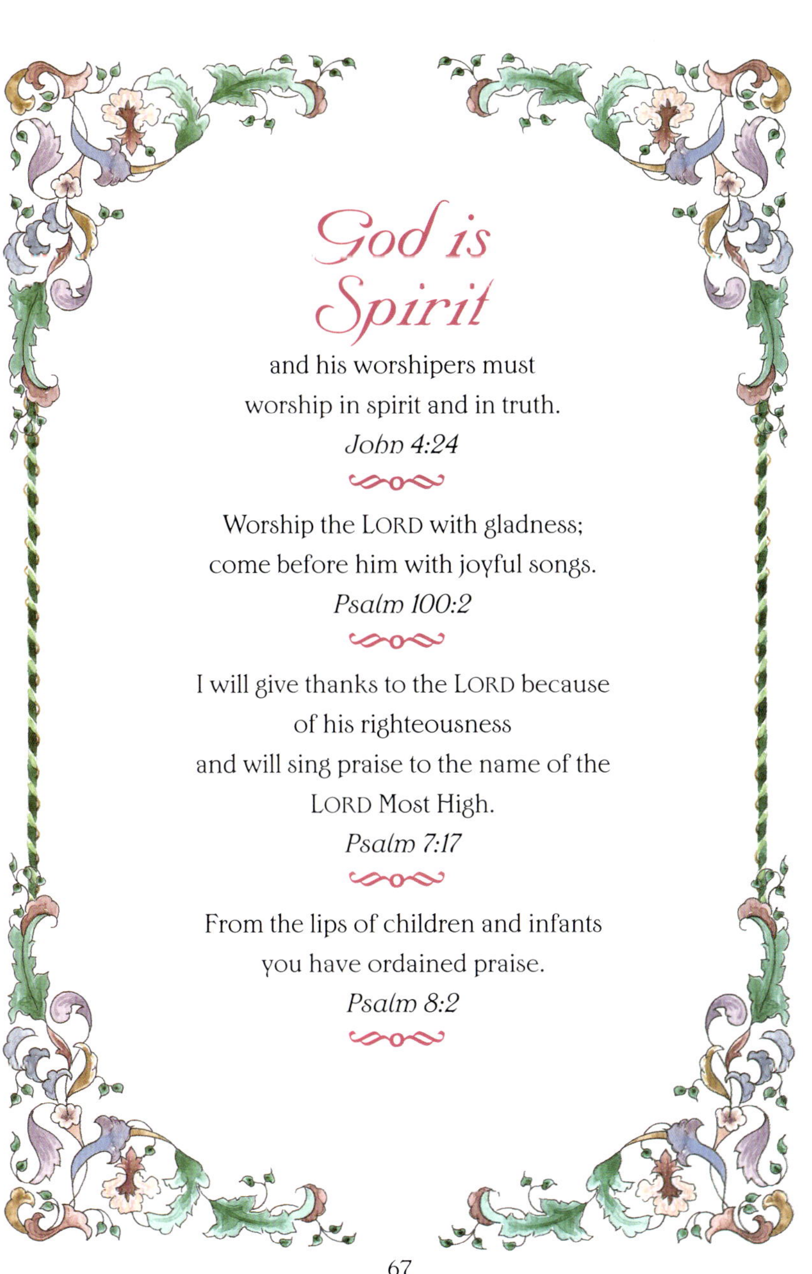

God is Spirit

and his worshipers must
worship in spirit and in truth.

John 4:24

Worship the LORD with gladness;
come before him with joyful songs.

Psalm 100:2

I will give thanks to the LORD because
of his righteousness
and will sing praise to the name of the
LORD Most High.

Psalm 7:17

From the lips of children and infants
you have ordained praise.

Psalm 8:2

To Be a Family

Is to love together, laugh together, cry together, and share the course of our lives with those who care about us.

It is to never face heartache alone, to freely rejoice at our blessings, and to share in the joy of the blessings of others.

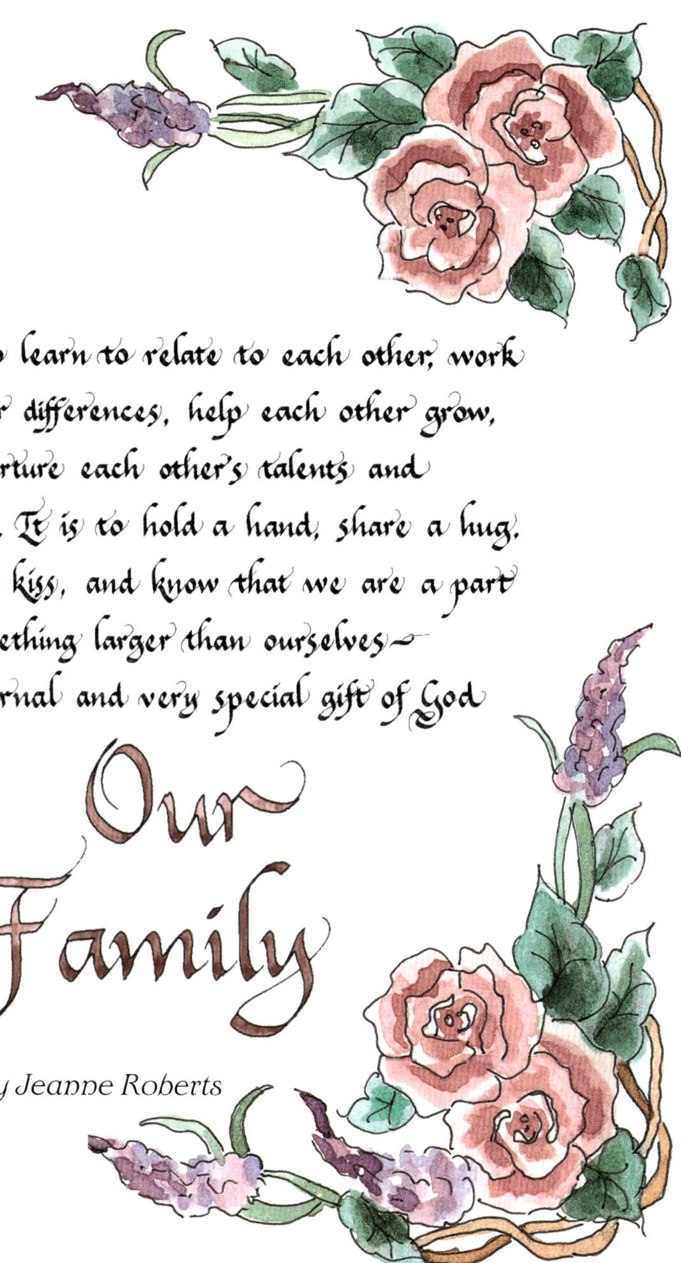

It is to learn to relate to each other, work out our differences, help each other grow, and nurture each other's talents and giftings. It is to hold a hand, share a hug, blow a kiss, and know that we are a part of something larger than ourselves—An eternal and very special gift of God called

Our Family

Audrey Jeanne Roberts

A Time of Rembrance and Thanksgiving

Today, it seems as though Thanksgiving has gotten lost in our culture. In fact, it seems to me that our culture has lost much in the ensuing years since my childhood. We've lost our innocence, our sense of wonder and gratitude. We've lost the knowledge that we need to give thanks to God for the riches we enjoy and the blessings he has bestowed upon us. A true celebration of this special holiday should reinforce those values in our homes and families.

I remember Thanksgiving when I was a little girl. For me it was a big event I looked forward to, not merely a holiday to fill the month between Halloween and Christmas.

My grandmother dried her leftover bread in the oven and saved it all year long for her wonderful stuffing that she put together the night before Thanksgiving. A day or two before that we would cook our own cranberry sauce and set it to chill in the refrigerator. The smell of pumpkin and apple pies filled the house.

I loved Thanksgiving because it meant that my aunt and uncle and their seven kids, my mom, my sister, my grandmother, and I all gathered into my grandmother's eight hundred square foot house! It was crowded, but that only served to heighten my joy in the holiday. Even though my cousins and I had to cram into Grandma's tiny kitchen and wash mountains of dirty dishes, we were happy with satisfied taste buds and full stomachs.

We spent all day together, talking, sharing, laughing, and caring for each other. I remember snippets of conversations between the adults as they cooked. I remember being constantly chased out of the kitchen and having my fingers swatted as I had a sneak preview of food to come. I remember going outside for games of chase and of hide-and-seek with the other kids as we waited seemingly endless hours for dinner.

I've come to realize that as wonderful as my memories of childhood are, back then we didn't really center on thankfulness either. Thankfulness is something I've had to learn. And only a thankful heart ever comes to know true contentment. It is so easy take for granted the gifts our heavenly Father has bestowed upon us. So in our family, in addition to creating memories for our children, we are working to emphasize a spirit of gratefulness and thanks.

Here's what we do.

We share every Thanksgiving with a different group of people. Sometimes we share with college students who are alone and far from home. Sometimes extended family members, or friends who've become like family to us, share with us. Some years we've had holidays with strangers or business acquaintances because we were out on the road and couldn't get home. But no matter where we are or who we're with, every holiday has been special because we carry the spirit of thanksgiving in our hearts.

Emphasize a spirit of thanks

One of our most treasured Thanksgiving traditions centers around my giant cobalt blue vase. On a slip of paper, we have each guest write his or her name, the year, and something for which he or she is especially thankful. Then we have them read their papers at the dinner table. We pull out a few of slips from prior years and read them as well. This tradition brings us back to where we were a year or a few years ago and helps us see how far we've come. It reminds us of the people who've shared with us in years past and builds our faith in the God of answered prayer. We may even read a slip of paper from a family member who's gone on to heaven before us.

Like a vase filled with white paper, your family might consider creating a special journal of thanksgiving. Let your children cut out pictures of turkeys, fall leaves, or anything else that remind them of Thanksgiving. Have each family member write in the book what he or she is grateful for and date it. Leave the book out all season long so that you can add to it. Then, when you are feeling down and need to be reminded of God's faithfulness in times past, you can pick it up and read through it. Your heart of thanksgiving will be renewed!

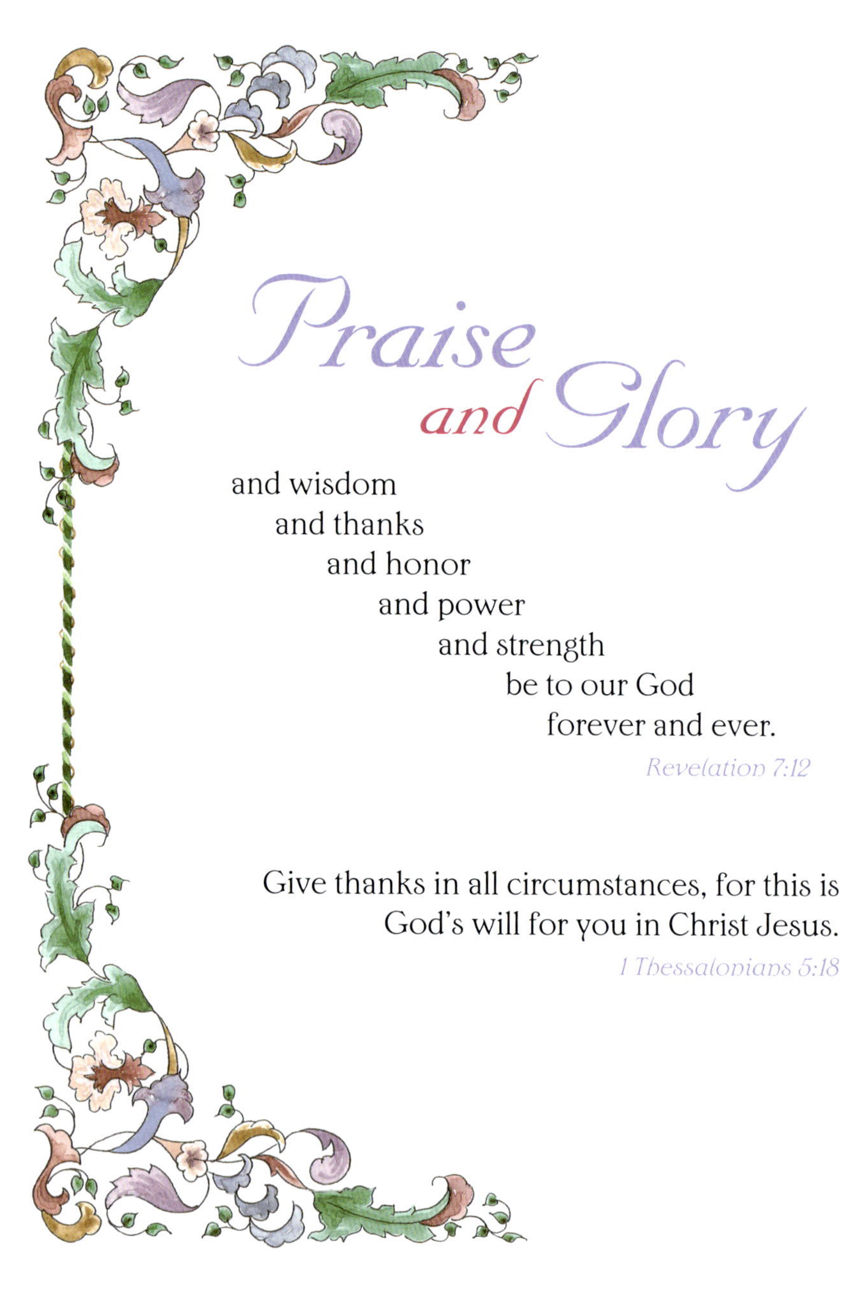

Praise *and* *Glory*

and wisdom
and thanks
and honor
and power
and strength
be to our God
forever and ever.

Revelation 7:12

Give thanks in all circumstances, for this is God's will for you in Christ Jesus.

1 Thessalonians 5:18

Speak to one another with
psalms,
hymns and
spiritual songs.

Sing and make music in your heart
to the Lord, always giving thanks
to God the Father for everything,
in the name of our Lord Jesus Christ.

Ephesians 5:19-20

I thank my God
every time I
remember you.

Philippians 1:3

Use Your Best Things

When I was growing up, we had a set of Rogers stainless flatware in a beautiful walnut, velvet-padded case. I believe a friend had given them to my mother as a gift. I recall asking several times on special family occasions if we could use the "good" silverware. The answer was always the same. "Those are for when company comes." I understand now, as an adult, that my mother never had the budget to be able to afford precious china or crystal, either as a single mom or later as a schoolteacher married to a man in the Navy.

The funny thing was, just before I left home she cleaned things out in preparation for a move to Florida, and she either gave that set of flatware away or sold it at a garage sale—and it had never once been used!

It's so easy for us to deny even ourselves the pleasure of using special things. But have you noticed that life is unpredictable? Before we know it much of life has passed us by and we are still waiting for an occasion to use our special things. I believe it is important to celebrate the everyday triumphs and joys of life and to use our special things.

When my girls were little, we were absolutely broke.

Their father and I had decided that it was more important for me to be at home with them than to work and bring in money for extras. So my household budget for gas, diapers, clothing, and food was only $50 per week. Even in 1981, that didn't go nearly far enough! But even in our impoverished financial state, I decided we would have a set of china and would use it for every special occasion, big or small.

Celebrate the everyday triumphs

Our local grocery store had a special offer on a pretty blue, silver, and white pattern that was very reasonably priced. I bought one piece at a time until I had a full set of twelve plates and bowls. My girls learned to carefully handle the dishes, wash them, and put them away because these were special dishes for special people—these plates were for them. I wanted my girls to know that they were even more special than the finest company who would ever come to visit. I also told them I understood accidents would happen and that was why I had bought a dozen plates! We had so much fun together setting up our elegant lunches or teas. The girls learned how to set the table. They also learned that we could celebrate their smallest triumphs from school by decorating our dinner table. Why, we could celebrate anything! We even celebrated the loss of a tooth!

Over the years, my girls and I bought beautiful pieces of silver and crystal at garage and estate sales. We learned how to take care of them and enjoyed using them without guilt, knowing that we had spent a tenth or less of their retail cost. The Lord honored our desire for beautiful things when our motives were right before him. We feel that he is the one who led us to fabulous finds at bargain-basement prices. One time he led us to an estate sale where we found five of the most beautiful, delicate, hand-cut crystal goblets—and they were only three dollars each. Fifteen dollars was a fortune to me at the time, but I knew the Lord wanted me to have those goblets. But by scrimping for a few weeks, we could have a lifetime to treasure them. I've been to a lot of antique shows since I purchased those goblets and have never yet found anything as exquisite. We used those priceless, precious goblets at my wedding to my second husband. God gives us all good and precious gifts. "Every good and perfect gift is from above, coming down from the Father of the heavenly lights, who does not change like shifting shadows" (James 1:17).

God gives us precious gifts

And the supermarket dishes? I still have the remnants of them. One day I will give a portion of them to each of my girls in remembrance of the special occasions we shared together as they were growing up.

What special things are you preserving? If you honestly examined your heart, would you have to admit that there is something you value more than your family members? Are you saving your special treasures to impress strangers at some unforeseen event, far in the future? There's nothing wrong with preserving priceless, irreplaceable items. To use delicate, easily-destroyed things, everyday, would be poor stewardship. As always, wisdom must find the balance, and that balance is in the attitude of the heart.

Special Ideas for the Family

1. Create a special award place setting. Go to a thrift store near you and find a beautiful or fun place setting of dishes. Or shop after Christmas sales for cream and gold plates with stars on them. (These can be your "Super Star" plates.) When a child or a family member accomplishes a goal, achieves a high grade, or simply completes a difficult school project on time, honor him or her regardless of the grade he or she gets. Make him or her the "Special Person of the Day."
2. Buy pressed glassware. It's inexpensive, and mixes and matches perfectly. You can find dinner plates,

dessert plates, glasses, serving bowls, and more at thrift shops for less than the cost of throw-away paper dinner plates. Then you can be ready for company or throw a family birthday party in minutes, and the dishes clean up easily in the dishwasher.

3. Buy vases at thrift shops that you can give away filled with flowers from your garden. You can also find florist's vases at garage sales all the time for a quarter or fifty cents. Chipped teacups and teapots can make beautiful containers for arrangements as well. Your floral gifts become even more special when a vase is part of the gift.
4. Buy a collection of odds-and-ends candleholders. We often found them at garages sales, especially silver-plated candelabras. Candlelight provides such a special atmosphere. The most ordinary things take on a beauty and emotional warmth. You can usually find candles on clearance after the holidays, and they aren't all red and green!

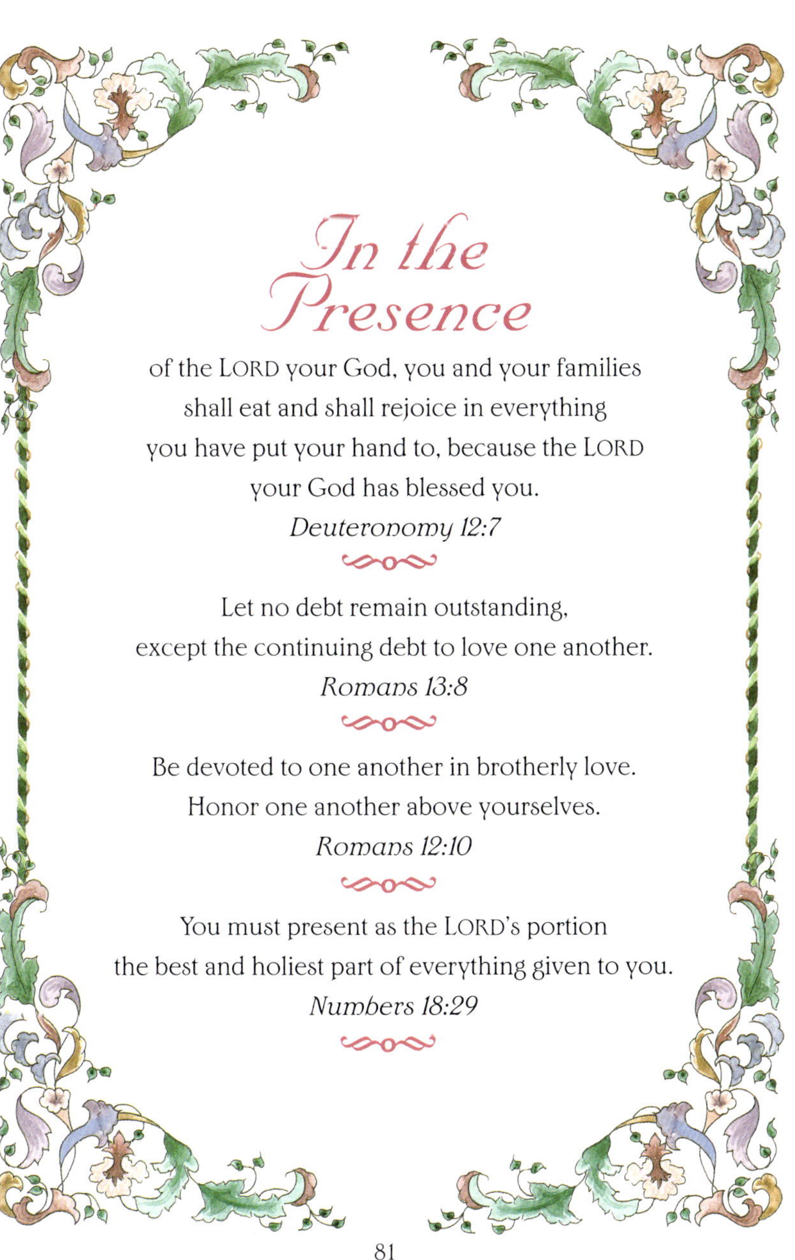

In the Presence

of the LORD your God, you and your families
shall eat and shall rejoice in everything
you have put your hand to, because the LORD
your God has blessed you.

Deuteronomy 12:7

Let no debt remain outstanding,
except the continuing debt to love one another.

Romans 13:8

Be devoted to one another in brotherly love.
Honor one another above yourselves.

Romans 12:10

You must present as the LORD's portion
the best and holiest part of everything given to you.

Numbers 18:29

Contentment...

Contentment can't
be bought nor sold
'Tis only made of
things of old.
Of child's smiles and joy-filled cries,
Of loving hugs and fond good-byes,
An attitude of heart... slow grown.
It's contentment makes a house a home.

Godliness with contentment
is great gain 1 Timothy 6:6

Audrey Jeanne Roberts

Share Your Home

Have you ever been the unexpected company that went to someone's door and then felt guilty because the hostess was so uncomfortable and apologetic about her home that you wished you'd never bothered her? It happened to me once and I realized that the person I was calling on was afraid of what I might be thinking about her. She was thinking about her home and I was thinking, "How can I make her feel more at ease and comfortable? I came to see her, not her house."

The most gracious way you can welcome a guest into your home–expected or unexpected–is to share your home with them, not show it off. Your home should reflect your family's lifestyle, tastes, passions, and interests. It should be a comfortable place to live, and not a place to photograph for magazines. What our lives are about should be evident in our environment. I love to look through a bookshelf and see what interests my friends. I love to see kids' artwork featured on refrigerators and to see handcrafted items they've made. Don't you?

In our 120-year-old farmhouse, we have a formal front entrance that no one uses. Everyone enters through my laundry room! It's a lovely room with lots of character, but when my laundry is piled up in what we affectionately call "Mount Roberts formation," there's no hiding it! We have the original "peeling-adobe-walls look" and we didn't even have to faux paint it to look like that. We still have unopened boxes from last year's move. Everywhere you look there are things that are undone, projects that need tackling, decorating to be undertaken. If we were to wait until we completed our home before we chose to have family or friends over, we'd lead a lonely life.

Welcome a guest into your home

This isn't to say that cleanliness and order aren't virtues. If a family is living in filth and squalor there is something deeply wrong. It's not okay to not care about cleanliness, sanitation, discipline, and order. But who among us has a happy, active, emotionally healthy, growing family and yet is capable of always maintaining a meticulously spotless house? Not me! Besides, standards of cleanliness in the home that are just short of passing a white glove test can lead to rebellion, resentment, and unhealthy family interactions. Balance is the key. If it's Saturday morning at your house and the dishes are still in the sink because you're reading the funny papers to each other and relaxing, your home is in balance.

My friend Sallylou once told me, "Because you are comfortable entertaining me with your dishes still in the sink, I can be comfortable having you over when my floor isn't vacuumed." Many of our most wonderful times of friendship have happened when I probably should have been cleaning my house, but instead stopped for several hours of conversation. Which do you think I value more, a clean house or the chatter with a friend?

Make your guests your focus

This is the secret of hospitality. *Make your guests your focus, not yourself or your home.* Love your guests, welcome them, make them comfortable, choose to be comfortable yourself, and you'll put them at ease and make wonderful memories.

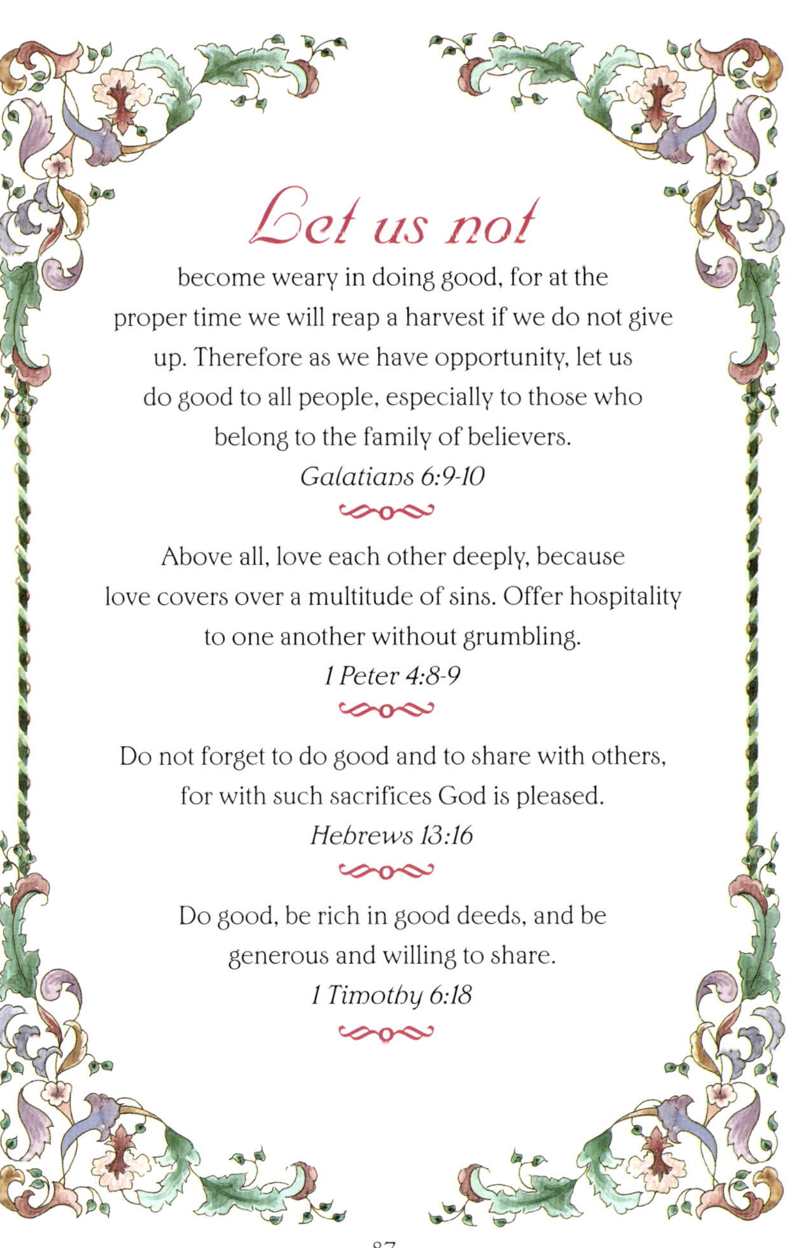

Let us not

become weary in doing good, for at the proper time we will reap a harvest if we do not give up. Therefore as we have opportunity, let us do good to all people, especially to those who belong to the family of believers.

Galatians 6:9-10

Above all, love each other deeply, because love covers over a multitude of sins. Offer hospitality to one another without grumbling.

1 Peter 4:8-9

Do not forget to do good and to share with others, for with such sacrifices God is pleased.

Hebrews 13:16

Do good, be rich in good deeds, and be generous and willing to share.

1 Timothy 6:18

In Times of Sorrow

There are few times in our lives where the love and support of our family will be more appreciated than during times of sorrow and loss.

My husband, after three-and-a-half years, finally lost his battle with cancer and the day arrived to hold his memorial service. It was a strange day when I felt as though I walked entirely alone and at the same time was held aloft by the love of my surrounding family.

At home after the service, all of my friends and family gathered to talk and to process our grief together. Some were overwhelmed and were unable to deal with the loss openly. It was too raw, too new. Some cried intensely, unable to believe that such a strong, seemingly healthy young man was gone. Others shared funny stories of Jim's youth, of how proud they were of his fight in his last days, and of how pleased they were that we shared the "real Jim" at his memorial—warts and all, not a whitewashed, prettied-up version.

As the day came to a close, I began to descend into a deep weariness that has no equal. Saying my good-byes, I started toward my bedroom to rest. Then out of the crowd someone suggested that a picture be taken that I never imagined in my wildest dreams could be taken—a picture of my sister and I with both our parents who had been divorced since I was eight. My parents had only been in the same room once or twice since the divorce. But that day, they had each been able to lay aside their personal hurt, discomfort, and pain to be there to help me through the roughest day of my life. That photograph helped me capture a lifetime memory.

Being a family often means setting aside personal needs or comforts to meet the needs of another family member. It means gathering together and sharing tears, burdens, and sorrows. Disasters and difficulties do not adhere to convenient schedules. No matter when they occur, it takes effort to come to the aid of those in our family who are affected. Successful families learn the skills of gathering around the one in deepest need, setting aside their own needs for a season and lending their strength, prayers, love, and encouragement. Successful families achieve the ability to lay aside misunderstandings, disagreements, bitterness, and anger in order to draw together in times of peril, disaster, or loss.

Being a family means sharing tears

Many extended families are unable to function in this manner. Yours may be one of them. You may have to set an example yourself and lead the way to change. The only reason I was blessed to have that treasured family photo of the four of us was because my father determined in his heart months before Jim's death that he would (with my stepfather's permission) take my mother aside and apologize to her for his failures as a husband. He took the first step, he shouldered the responsibility, and his thoughtfulness facilitated a peaceful, even joyful reunion. I had the photo because my family loved me enough to be there for me.

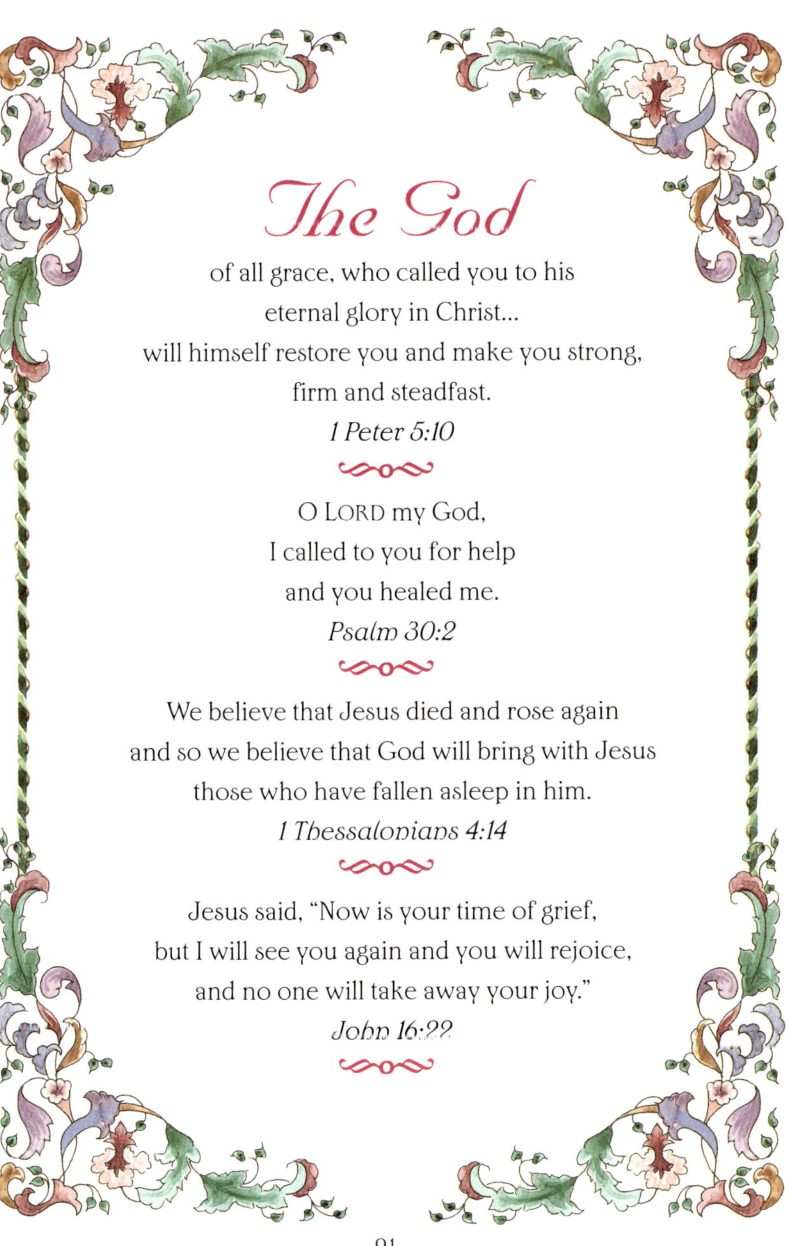

The God

of all grace, who called you to his
eternal glory in Christ...
will himself restore you and make you strong,
firm and steadfast.

1 Peter 5:10

O LORD my God,
I called to you for help
and you healed me.

Psalm 30:2

We believe that Jesus died and rose again
and so we believe that God will bring with Jesus
those who have fallen asleep in him.

1 Thessalonians 4:14

Jesus said, "Now is your time of grief,
but I will see you again and you will rejoice,
and no one will take away your joy."

John 16:22

Savoring the Moment

How many of the special moments in your life did you realize were special at the time they were happening? How many of those moments grew in value in your mind and heart later—when you realized they could never be repeated?

When I think of our extended family, I often think about all the weddings we've attended. Those family weddings punctuate the passage of time like mile markers on a highway. When we were small, all my cousins and I would play together at family gatherings. Then before you knew it, we all got married. Very soon we were watching each other's children playing at family gatherings just like we used to do. Now, those children have grown, and one by one they are getting married and starting families of their own.

I remember wanting to slow down on my own wedding day, to expand the seconds and extend the day. Almost all the people I loved were in one room at one time! How incredibly precious it was. Would we ever be together like this again? I knew that someday I would look at our wedding photos and see faces captured there that were no longer with us. I knew that life would continue to unfold in unpredictable, often uncontrollable ways, and I wanted to remember the sweetness of the day. I wanted so much to talk to every person there and to treasure his or her presence with me. But no matter how hard I tried to slow it down, the day raced by.

As a young mother, I listened to older mothers around me and I heard one consistent phrase from all of them "Enjoy every day with your babies because they change so fast you won't believe it. They grow too fast!"

Enjoy every day? How could I do that when I was up to my elbows in diapers, baby food jars, laundry, and spit up? How could I live my life so that when my child was grown, I could say that I had enjoyed every moment to its fullest? I prayed, "Lord, help me treasure this moment with my child. Help me recognize the uniqueness of each day and value the time we spend together. Help me remember what these days were like, what she was like ... Lord, help me."

> Recognize the gift and offer thanks

Then God showed me a secret. I could capture memories and store them up like priceless treasures when I took time to be thankful for them. Gratefulness, thanksgiving, appreciation–these are the collectors of memories. We just have to pause for a moment to recognize the gift and offer thanks.

We just have to open our eyes and hearts to see the richness that sits right before us. The secret is being content with what is. It is accepting what happens—even if things don't go the way we planned. It is choosing to delight in the moment.

I also discovered that it is almost impossible to adopt these attitudes (contentment, acceptance, delight) without slowing down. Only when I put on the brakes; stopped my frantic, racing thoughts; and disciplined myself did I learn to be thankful.

If you are waiting for perfect "Norman Rockwell" moments in your life, complete with soft lighting, background music, and "heavenly mist," you'll wait forever! Norman Rockwell's genius was that he caught moments that were simply slices of everyday life. They were moments that passed millions of us right by until he captured them for us. How did he do it? He recognized the moment. He appreciated the moment. He savored the moment enough to record it for all time.

You and I can't stop time. We can't freeze the action or bring back a certain moment at will. Oh that we could! But in learning to consciously pause, to drink in the details of what we see and hear, to express what we feel to those we love, and to give thanks to the Lord in the midst of all his blessings, we will learn the fine art of *savoring the moment.*

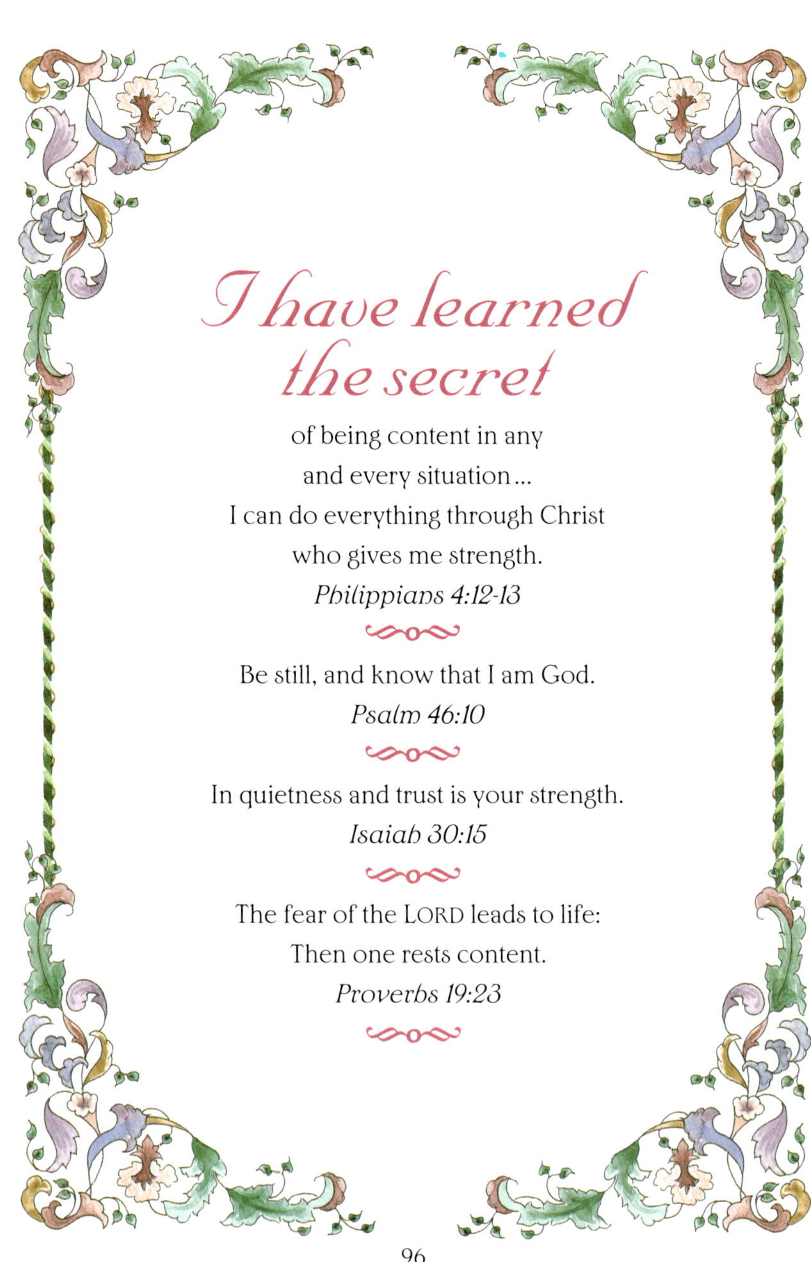

I have learned the secret

of being content in any
and every situation...
I can do everything through Christ
who gives me strength.
Philippians 4:12-13

Be still, and know that I am God.
Psalm 46:10

In quietness and trust is your strength.
Isaiah 30:15

The fear of the LORD leads to life:
Then one rests content.
Proverbs 19:23